Write Your Own Adventure Book

How to Master Plot Twists for Teens: Fiction Writing Guide for Beginners

DR. FANATOMY

GIFT FOR TEEN

copyright@ dr. fanatomy 2025

All rights reserved. No part of this publication may be reproduced, distributed, or transmitted in any form or by any means, including photocopying, recording, or other electronic or mechanical methods, without the prior written permission of the publisher, except in the case of brief quotations embodied in critical reviews and certain other noncommercial uses permitted by copyright law.

This book is a work of non-fiction, and any resemblance to actual persons, living or dead, or actual events is purely coincidental.

The information and techniques described in this book are intended for educational and informational purposes only. The author and publisher shall not be held liable for any injury, damage, or loss arising from using or misusing the information presented in this book.

While every effort has been made to ensure the accuracy of the information contained within this book, the author and publisher make no warranties or representations express or implied, about the completeness, accuracy, reliability, suitability, or availability with respect to the contents of this book for any purpose. The use of any information provided in this book is at the reader's own risk.

TABLE OF CONTENTS

CHAPTER 1: BOOK INTRODUCTION: WHY ADVENTURE WRITING MATTERS FOR TEENS

(Pg:3-7)

- Your Journey Starts Here
- Why Writing Adventures Rocks
- The Power of Storytelling
- Table: How Stories Help You Shine
- Why Adventure Stories Spark Creativity
- Mind Map: Adventure Story Ideas
- Building Confidence Through Writing
- Your First Adventure Starts Now!

CHAPTER 2: PLOT TWISTS: THE SECRET TO EPIC ADVENTURES

(Pg: 8-16)

- Why Plot Twists Make Adventures Epic
- What Makes a Plot Twist Unforgettable?
- Learning from YA Twist Masters
- Avoiding Predictable Adventure Plots
- Table: Clichés to Avoid and Fresh Fixes
- Chapter Wrap-Up
- Activity Zone and Answers

TABLE OF CONTENTS

CHAPTER 3: CHARACTERS THAT POWER YOUR TWISTS
(Pg: 17-25)

- Why Characters Make or Break Twists
- Crafting Relatable Heroes
- Table: Building a Relatable Hero
- Flowchart: Hero's Conflict to Twist
- Side Characters with Surprise Power
- Mind Map: Side Character Twists
- Villains with Depth
- Crafting Villains That Pop
- Favorite Characters for American Teens
- Chapter Wrap-Up
- Activity Zone and Answers

CHAPTER 4: MASTERING ADVENTURE PLOT STRUCTURE
(Pg: 26-35)

- Why Structure Is Your Storytelling Superpower
- Beginning, Middle, and End
- Flowchart: Three-Act Adventure Structure
- Where to Place Twists
- Keeping the Story Moving
- Table: Balancing Story Elements
- Table: Favorite Stories for American Teens
- Chapter Wrap-Up
- Activity Zone and Answers

TABLE OF CONTENTS

CHAPTER 5: FROM SPARK TO ADVENTURE: BRAINSTORMING IDEAS

(Pg: 36-45)

- Why Brainstorming Is a Writer's Superpower
- Finding Inspiration Everywhere
- Table: Turning Life into Story Seeds
- Flowchart: Spark to Story
- Prompts and Games for Creativity
- Table: Organizing Tools
- Table: Favorite Story Ideas for Teens
- Chapter Wrap-Up
- Activity Zone and Answers

CHAPTER 6: WRITING TRICKS TO HOOK READERS

(Pg: 46-55)

- Why Writing Tricks Hook Readers
- Building Suspense and Mystery
- Flowchart: Building Suspense to Twist
- Dialogue That Drops Hints
- Mind Map: Dialogue for Twists
- Balancing Action with Emotion
- Table: Action vs. Emotion
- Favorite Stories for Teens
- Chapter Wrap-Up
- Activity Zone and Answers

TABLE OF CONTENTS

CHAPTER 7: BEATING WRITER'S BLOCK AND STAYING PUMPED
(Pg: 56 -65)

- Normalizing Writer's Block for Teens
- Why Writer's Block Happens
- Flowchart: Why You're Stuck
- Fun Fixes for Stuck Moments
- Mind Map: Fixes for Writer's Block
- Finding Motivation Through Community
- Table: Community Motivation
- Motivational Tips from Favorite Characters
- Table: Motivational Tips from Favorite Characters
- Chapter Wrap-Up
- Activity Zone and Answers

CHAPTER 8: PUTTING IT ALL TOGETHER: WRITING YOUR ADVENTURE STORIES
(Pg: 66 -82)

- Why This Chapter Is Your Story-Writing Workout
- Story 1: The Cursed Compass Quest
- Story 2: The Hidden Portal Betrayal
- Story 3: The Shadow Monster Chase
- Story 4: The Forgotten Kingdom Heist
- Story 5: The Time Loop Trap
- Story 6: The Rebel Alliance Secret
- Story 7: The Enchanted Forest Mystery
- Story 8: The Underwater Treasure Betrayal
- Story 9: The Space Station Sabotage
- Story 10: The Lost Artifact Revelation
- Answers: Sample Stories

TABLE OF CONTENTS

CONCLUSION (Pg: 83-84)

- Your Adventure Awaits: Keep Writing, Keep Twisting

APPENDIX (Pg: 85-88)

- Appendix -A: Plot Twist Types and Placement Guide
- Appendix -B: Character Creation Quick-Reference Template
- Appendix - C: Three-Act Structure Checklist
- Appendix - D: Brainstorming and Hooking Tools at a Glance
- Appendix - E: Beating Block & Sharing Your Stories

Chapter 1: Why Adventure Writing Matters for Teens

Your Journey Starts Here

Hey, teen writer! Ever dreamed of battling dragons, exploring haunted jungles, or outsmarting a cunning villain? That's the magic of adventure stories—and you can create them! Writing your own adventure isn't just about making cool stories; it's about discovering who you are, sharing your voice, and building confidence to take on the world. This chapter is your launchpad to see why writing adventures is a total game-changer for teens like you. Ready to jump in? Let's go!

In this chapter, you'll find out why writing adventures lets you explore, dream, and grow. We'll talk about how stories help you express your unique voice and connect with others. Plus, we'll show you how adventure stories spark your creativity and build courage—complete with examples, a table, and a mind map to get your ideas flowing. Oh, and there's a fun activity to kick off your writing quest!

Why Writing Adventures Rocks

Writing adventure stories is like grabbing a ticket to any world you want—without leaving your room. It's a chance to express what makes you you, from your wildest dreams to your deepest feelings. Whether you're into epic quests like The Hunger Games or survival tales like Hatchet, adventure stories let you explore big ideas, connect with others, and grow stronger. Here's why it's so awesome:

- Explore: Create worlds where anything's possible—flying ships, secret portals, or talking wolves!
- Express: Share your thoughts, fears, or hopes through characters who feel real.
- Grow: Writing stories develops skills like problem-solving and confidence that benefit students in school and life.

Quick Example: Think of Katniss Everdeen in The Hunger Games. Her story isn't just about survival; it's about standing up for what's right. When you write your own adventure, you get to decide what your hero stands for—maybe something you care about, like friendship or justice.

The Power of Storytelling

Stories are like superpowers for teens. They let you share your emotions, test crazy ideas, and even shape the world. Whether it's a TikTok skit, a Wattpad novel, or a movie script, teen voices are everywhere in media today. Writing your own adventure story gives you a safe space to say what's on your mind and connect with others who get it.

Why Stories Matter

- Share Emotions and Identity: Stories let you pour out your feelings—anger, joy, or confusion—through characters. Maybe your hero's dealing with a tough family situation, just like you.
- Safe Space for Ideas: Want to imagine a world without homework or where teens rule? Writing lets you try out ideas without real-world risks.
- Teen Voices in Media: Look at Stranger Things—created by adults but inspired by teen adventures. Your stories could inspire someone, too!

Table: How Stories Help You Shine

What Stories Do	How It Helps You	Example
Share Emotions	Turn feelings into characters or plots	A hero who's shy but saves the day, like you at school
Test Ideas	Try out wild "what ifs" safely	What if you found a secret map in your backyard?
Connect with Others	Reach readers who feel the same	Share a story about friendship on Wattpad

Example: In Percy Jackson, Rick Riordan created Percy, a teen who feels like an outsider but discovers he's a demigod. Writing a character like that lets you explore your own feelings of being different—and connect with readers who feel the same.

Activity: Write a 100-word scene about a teen hero facing a tough choice. Maybe they're deciding whether to sneak out for an adventure or stay safe. Use it to show an emotion you've felt lately.

Why Adventure Stories Spark Creativity

Adventure stories are like rocket fuel for your imagination. They're all about bold quests, daring escapes, and epic battles—think Harry Potter dodging Voldemort or The Mandalorian protecting Baby Yoda. These stories don't just entertain; they push you to dream bigger and create worlds that feel alive.

How Adventures Fire Up Your Brain

- Inspire Creativity: Adventure stories let you invent crazy worlds, like jungles with glowing plants or cities in the clouds.
- Escape vs. Truth: Adventures let you escape reality (school stress, anyone?) while exploring real truths, such as standing up to bullies or finding the courage to do so.
- Famous Examples: Books like The Hobbit or games like The Legend of Zelda show how adventures make teens dream big—your story could do that, too!

Mind Map: Adventure Story Ideas

[Adventure Story]
    ├── World: (Jungle, Space, Haunted School)
    ├── Hero: (Shy teen, Rebel, Secret Genius)
    ├── Goal: (Find treasure, Save friend, Stop villain)
    ├── Twist: (Friend is a traitor, Map is fake, Hero has powers)

Example: In The Hobbit, Bilbo Baggins starts as a cozy hobbit but ends up facing a dragon. That journey sparks creativity because it's about stepping out of your comfort zone—something you can do by writing an adventure!

Activity: List 3 adventure stories (books, movies, games) you love and 1 thing you'd change in each. For example, "In The Hunger Games, I'd give Peeta a secret skill to surprise Katniss." This gets you thinking like a storyteller.

Building Confidence Through Writing

Writing an adventure story is like slaying a dragon—it's tough, but when you finish, you feel unstoppable. Every word you write builds courage, helps you face fears, and makes your voice stronger. Whether it's a short story or a full novel, you're proving you can create something amazing.

Why Writing Makes You Stronger

- Finishing Builds Courage: Completing a story, even a short one, shows you can tackle big challenges.
- Facing Fears: Writing about a hero facing danger (like a dark forest or a betraying friend) lets you work through your own worries.
- Storytelling vs. Journaling: Journaling is great for private thoughts, but storytelling shares your ideas with the world, amplifying your voice.

Example: In Six of Crows, Kaz Brekker faces his fears to pull off an impossible heist. Writing a character like Kaz lets you explore your own challenges—like standing up to a tough teacher or trying something new.

Activity: Write a 50-word moment where a character overcomes self-doubt. Maybe they're about to enter a mysterious cave but hesitate. Show how they push forward. This helps you practice writing courage—and feel it yourself!

Your First Adventure Starts Now!

You're not just reading this book—you're starting an epic quest to write your own adventure. Every chapter will give you tools to craft plot twists, build characters, and share stories that wow readers. Ready to take the first step? Try this activity to spark your imagination.

Activity: Write a 50-word "What if" adventure idea. Example: "What if a teen finds a glowing compass that teleports them to a pirate ship?" Keep it short, wild, and full of possibility. This is your first step to becoming an adventure-writing hero!

Chapter 2 : Plot Twists: The Secret to Epic Adventures

Chapter 2 – Plot Twists: The Secret to Epic Adventures

Hey, teen writer! Ever had your mind blown by a story twist that flipped everything you thought you knew? Like, the hero's best friend turns out to be the bad guy, or the whole adventure was a setup? That's the power of a plot twist—the ultimate trick to make your adventure story unforgettable. In this chapter, you'll learn how to craft twists that shock readers, keep them hooked, and make your story as epic as The Hunger Games or Stranger Things. Ready to level up your writing? Let's dive in!

We'll explore why plot twists are the heartbeat of awesome fiction, what makes them stick, how YA pros like Percy Jackson pull them off, and how to avoid lame, predictable plots. With examples, tables, a mind map, and fun activities, you'll be dropping jaw-dropping twists in no time. Plus, there's a beefed-up quiz at the end to test your skills. Buckle up for the ride!

Why Plot Twists Make Adventures Epic

Plot twists are like a rollercoaster drop—they surprise readers, crank up suspense, and make your adventure impossible to put down. Whether it's a secret villain or a quest gone wrong, twists keep readers guessing, "What's gonna happen next?" Here's why they're a game-changer:

- Surprise: Twists flip the script, making readers gasp, "No way!"
- Suspense: They keep every page exciting, like a cliffhanger in a Netflix show.
- Heartbeat of Fiction: Twists give your story life, turning a basic tale into an epic adventure.

Example: In Stranger Things, when we learn Barb's fate, it's a twist that hits hard because we care about her. Your twists can do that, too, making readers feel every shock.

Activity: Brainstorm 3 unexpected twists for a story about a lost explorer. Example: "The explorer's guide is secretly leading them to a trap." Write them down to spark your next big idea!

What Makes a Plot Twist Unforgettable?

A killer plot twist isn't just a random surprise—it's a shock that feels right when it lands. It has to wow readers, hit them in the feels, and be backed by clever clues. Let's break down the must-haves for a twist that sticks.

Ingredients for an Epic Twist

- Shock vs. Cheap Tricks: A great twist is surprising but makes sense (like a trusted ally turning traitor), not lazy (like "It was all a dream"—ugh, hard pass). Readers should think, "Whoa, but yeah, I get it!"
- Emotional Stakes: Twists hurt or thrill more when readers care about your characters. A sibling's betrayal stings if we love their bond.
- Planting Clues: Drop sneaky hints early so the twist feels fair, like puzzle pieces clicking into place.

Table: Epic Twist vs. Lame Twist

Feature	Epic Twist	Lame Twist
Surprise	Shocking but logical (e.g., mentor's a villain)	Random, no setup (e.g., aliens appear)
Emotion	Hits the feels (e.g., friend's betrayal)	No stakes (e.g., stranger was evil)
Clues	Subtle hints (e.g., mentor's shifty eyes)	No foreshadowing (e.g., "It was a joke!")

Example: In The Hunger Games, Peeta's fake alliance with the Careers shocks Katniss and us. It works because we care about their trust, and clues (Peeta's subtle glances) hint he's playing a bigger game. Your twists need that setup and heart!

Prompt: Write a 100-word scene with a subtle clue to a later twist. Example: Your hero notices their guide clutching a weird amulet ,but shrugs it off—later, it's a villain's symbol. Keep the clue sneaky but clear enough to connect.

Learning from YA Twist Masters

Want to write twists like the pros? YA books like Percy Jackson, Six of Crows, and Harry Potter are packed with surprises that keep teens glued to the page. Let's steal their secrets to make your story pop!

Why These Twists Rule

- **Reader Trust:** Authors make you love characters, so twists feel like a punch to the gut.
- **Surprise + Clues**: Twists shock but make sense when you look back at the hints.
- **Your Takeaway:** Build trust and drop subtle clues to craft twists readers rave about.

Mind Map: Crafting a YA Plot Twist

[Plot Twist]
    ├── *Setup: (Hints in dialogue, actions, objects)*
    ├── *Trigger: (Event that sparks the twist, e.g., finding a secret)*
    ├── *Reveal: (The big "whoa" moment, e.g., "They're the enemy!")*
    ├── *Payoff: (How it changes the story or hero)*

Examples:

1. **Percy Jackson:** The Lightning Thief – Twist: Luke, a camp buddy, betrays Percy to Kronos. Why it works: Luke's grumpy comments (clues) and Percy's trust make the reveal a total shock.
2. **Six of Crows** – Twist: Kaz's heist hides a secret plan to save Inej. Why it works: Kaz's sly remarks hint at deeper motives, keeping you hooked.
3. **Harry Potter and the Goblet of Fire** – Twist: Professor Moody is Barty Crouch Jr. in disguise. Why it works: Moody's weird actions (clues) and Harry's danger make it a game-changer.

Activity: Rewrite a famous twist from a YA book in your own words (100 words). Example: Retell Luke's betrayal from Percy Jackson with your characters. Maybe your hero trusts a teammate who's secretly sabotaging their mission. Make it yours!

Avoiding Predictable Adventure Plots

Nothing tanks an adventure faster than a plot readers can guess from the first page. Clichés like "chosen one saves the world" or "evil overlord wants power" are so overdone that they bore teens who've binged Star Wars or Marvel. Let's keep your story fresh and surprising!

Tricks to Stay Unpredictable

- Dodge Clichés: Skip tired tropes like "prophecy kid" or "cartoon villain" unless you add a unique spin.
- Bend Expectations: Shock with role reversals (e.g., the sidekick's the real hero) or hidden motives (e.g., the quest's a trap).
- Timing Twists: Drop surprises at unexpected moments, like mid-story or during a calm scene.

Table: Clichés to Avoid and Fresh Fixes

Cliché	Why It's Boring	Fresh Twist
Chosen one saves world	Too obvious (e.g., *Star Wars*)	The "chosen one" is a fake; a nobody steps up
Evil overlord	No depth (e.g., cartoon bad guys)	Villain's fighting for a cause the hero understands
Happy ending, no cost	Feels flat, no stakes	Hero wins but loses something big (e.g., a friend)

Example: In The Maze Runner, the "haven" being another test avoids the cliché "everyone's saved" ending. It keeps readers on edge with a darker twist. You can do this by making your hero's goal (e.g., finding a treasure) hide a secret (e.g., it's cursed).

Prompt: Write a 50-word twist where the hero's best friend has a secret agenda. Example: Your hero trusts their friend to guide them through a desert, but the friend's leading them to a bandit's ambush. Keep it short and shocking!

Chapter Wrap-Up

Plot twists are your secret weapon for crafting adventures that teens can't stop reading. By surprising readers, building emotional stakes, and sneaking in clever clues, you'll create stories as epic as Percy Jackson or Six of Crows. Use these tricks—dodge clichés, learn from YA masters, and practice with our prompts—to make your twists pop. Now, hit the quiz below to see if you're a twist master!

ACTIVITY ZONE

ACTIVITY 1 - MULTIPLE CHOICE QUESTIONS

1) What makes a plot twist memorable?
a) It's completely random with no setup
b) It surprises readers but feels earned with clues
c) It repeats the same twist multiple times
d) It avoids any emotional connection

2) Which YA book features a twist where a friend betrays the hero?
a) The Hunger Games
b) Percy Jackson: The Lightning Thief
c) Harry Potter and the Sorcerer's Stone
d) The Maze Runner

3) Why are emotional stakes crucial for a plot twist?
a) They make the twist harder to write
b) They make readers care about the surprise
c) They confuse readers with too many feelings
d) They slow down the story's pace

4) What's a good way to avoid predictable plots?
a) Use clichés like "evil overlord" every time
b) Drop twists only at the very end
c) Use role reversals or hidden motives
d) Make every character predictable

5) How should you plant clues for a plot twist?
a) Make them super obvious so readers guess it
b) Drop subtle hints that connect later
c) Avoid clues entirely for maximum shock
d) Explain the twist right before it happens

ACTIVITY ZONE

ACTIVITY 2 – TRUE/FALSE QUESTIONS

1. **True or False:** A plot twist should always be predictable to keep readers comfortable.
2. **True or False:** Emotional stakes make plot twists hit harder for readers.
3. **True or False:** Clichés like "chosen one" always make a story more exciting.
4. **True or False:** Dropping a twist in a quiet moment can surprise readers more.
5. **True or False:** In Six of Crows, Kaz's twist involves a secret plan to save Inej.

ACTIVITY 3 – FILL-IN-THE-BLANK QUESTIONS

1. A great plot twist needs subtle _____ to make it feel logical when revealed.
2. In The Hunger Games, Peeta's _____ with the Careers is a shocking twist.
3. To avoid clichés, use _____ reversals to surprise readers.
4. In Harry Potter and the Goblet of Fire, the twist reveals Moody is _____ in disguise.
5. A twist with no emotional _____ feels flat and forgettable.

🎯 ACTIVITY ZONE

ACTIVITY 4 – MATCH THE FOLLOWING

Book	Plot Twist
A. Percy Jackson: The Lightning Thief	1. A heist hides a secret rescue plan
B. Six of Crows	2. A mentor is a villain in disguise
C. Harry Potter and the Goblet of Fire	3. A friend betrays the hero
D. The Maze Runner	4. The safe haven is another test
E. The Hunger Games	5. An ally pretends to join the enemy

ACTIVITY 5 – ANSWER QUESTIONS

1. In 50 words, create a plot twist for an adventure story where the hero discovers something shocking about their quest. Example: The hero's map to a treasure is a trap set by their lost sibling.
2. In 30 words, describe a clue you'd plant for a twist where the hero's guide is a traitor. Example: The guide keeps checking a strange watch that glows faintly.
3. In 30 words, explain why "It was all a dream" is a bad twist. Example: It's random, ignores clues, and frustrates readers by making the story feel pointless.
4. In 50 words, rewrite a twist from Six of Crows with your own characters. Example: Your leader's plan to steal a gem hides their goal to free a trapped friend.
5. In 30 words, describe a role reversal twist for an adventure story. Example: The nerdy sidekick, not the hero, is the true leader destined to stop the villain.

ANSWERS
🎯 ACTIVITY ZONE

(Use these to spark ideas, but make your answers 100% you!)

ACTIVITY 1: MULTIPLE CHOICE QUESTIONS

1. b) It surprises readers but feels earned with clues
2. b) Percy Jackson: The Lightning Thief
3. b) They make readers care about the surprise
4. c) Use role reversals or hidden motives
5. b) Drop subtle hints that connect later

ACTIVITY 2: TRUE/FALSE QUESTIONS

1. False (Twists should surprise, not be predictable)
2. True
3. False (Clichés make stories predictable, not exciting)
4. True
5. True

ACTIVITY 3: FILL-IN-THE-BLANK ANSWERS

1. Clues
2. Alliance
3. Role
4. Barty Crouch Jr.
5. Stakes

ACTIVITY 4: MATCH THE FOLLOWING

1. A-3 (Percy Jackson: Luke betrays Percy)
2. B-1 (Six of Crows: Kaz's secret rescue plan)
3. C-2 (Harry Potter: Moody is Barty Crouch Jr.)
4. D-4 (The Maze Runner: Safe haven is a test)
5. E-5 (The Hunger Games: Peeta pretends to join Careers)

ACTIVITY 5: SHORT-ANSWER QUESTIONS

1. Sample Answer: The hero's quest to find a lost city reveals it's a prison run by their missing dad, who's alive and guarding a secret weapon. They must join or stop him. (50 words)
2. Sample Answer: The guide nervously hides a coded note in their bag, glancing at it when the hero's distracted. (30 words)
3. Sample Answer: "It was all a dream" is bad because it's random, lacks clues, and frustrates readers by making the story feel pointless and emotionally empty. (30 words)
4. Sample Answer: My leader's plan to steal a crown hides their mission to free their trapped sister from a dungeon, revealed when they ditch the crown for a jail key. (50 words)
5. Sample Answer: The shy sidekick, not the bold hero, is the prophesied warrior destined to defeat the villain, revealed when they wield a hidden power. (30 words)

Chapter 3: Characters That Power Your Twists

CHAPTER 3 –Characters That Power Your Twists

Yo, teen writer! Plot twists are awesome, but without characters readers care about, they're like a fireworks show with no spark. Think Katniss in The Hunger Games—her grit makes every twist hit hard. Your heroes, sidekicks, and villains are the heart of your adventure, powering twists that leave readers shaken. In this chapter, you'll learn how to craft characters so real they leap off the page and make your twists epic, like in Percy Jackson or Stranger Things. Ready to build your dream squad? Let's dive in!

We'll explore why characters make or break twists, how to create relatable heroes, surprising sidekicks, and villains with depth. With examples, tables, a flowchart, mind maps, and fun prompts, you'll craft characters that pop. We'll wrap with a table of favorite characters American teens love, plus a quiz to test your skills. Oh, and we'll tie in the Free Character Profile Template to make your characters next-level. Let's get started!

Why Characters Make or Break Twists

A plot twist is only as good as the characters it's tied to. If readers don't love (or love to hate) your hero, sidekick, or villain, your twist—no matter how clever—falls flat. Characters make twists feel personal, like a bestie's betrayal or a villain's secret motive. Here's why they're the secret sauce:

- Emotional Connection: Readers need to care about your characters to feel the twist's punch.
- Twist Drivers: Characters' secrets, flaws, or choices spark the best surprises.
- Adventure Fuel: Heroes, sidekicks, and villains keep your story rolling with their decisions.

Example: In Six of Crows, Kaz's secret plan to save Inej shocks us because we're hooked on their bond. Your characters can do that, too, making twists hit like a tidal wave!

Activity: Sketch a character hiding a secret (use the bonus template). Example: A shy teen who's secretly a werewolf. Jot down their name, secret, and how they hide it using the Free Character Profile Template (more on that later!).

Crafting Relatable Heroes

Your hero is your story's star, but perfect heroes are boring! Relatable heroes have flaws, goals, and struggles that feel real, like teens you know. These traits set up awesome twists when their inner conflicts lead to surprises.

Making Heroes Real
- Flaws: Heroes need weaknesses, like being too impulsive or scared of failing, to feel human.
- Goals: Clear goals (e.g., save a friend, find a lost city) drive the adventure and set up twists.
- Struggles: Inner conflicts (e.g., guilt, self-doubt) can spark external surprises, like a bad choice that flips the plot.

Table: Building a Relatable Hero

Trait	Why It Matters	Example
Flaw	Makes the hero human	Percy Jackson's loyalty often leads him into trouble
Goal	Drives the story	Katniss Everdeen's main goal is to protect her sister Prim
Struggle	Sets up twists	Harry Potter's fear of becoming like Voldemort creates inner conflict

Flowchart: Hero's Conflict to Twist

[Hero's Inner Conflict] → [Bad Choice or Secret Revealed] → [Plot Twist]
Example: Self-doubt → Hides a secret power → Power saves the day

Example: In Percy Jackson, Percy's loyalty (flaw) makes him trust Luke, setting up the twist when Luke betrays him. His struggle (feeling like an outsider) makes the twist sting. Your hero's flaws can spark twists, too!

Prompt: Write a 100-word scene where your hero's flaw causes trouble. Example: Your hero's recklessness makes them charge into a cave, triggering a trap. Show how their flaw messes things up!

Side Characters with Surprise Power

Side characters—like best friends or quirky allies—aren't just backup dancers. They can spark massive twists with their loyalty, betrayal, or hidden skills. A sidekick who seems minor can flip your story upside down!

Sidekicks That Steal the Show

- Loyalty Twists: A loyal friend might hide a secret to protect the hero, leading to a twist.
- Betrayal Twists: A sidekick turning traitor can shock readers (ouch!).
- Hidden Skills: A quiet ally revealing a superpower or secret past can change everything.

Mind Map: Side Character Twists

[Side Character]
├── Loyalty: (Hides a secret to help the hero)
├── Betrayal: (Works for the villain)
├── Hidden Skill: (Reveals a talent, e.g., hacking)
├── Twist Impact: (Changes hero's quest or trust)

Example: In Stranger Things, Dustin's loyalty to Dart (the baby Demogorgon) sets up a twist when Dart turns dangerous. His unexpected bond flips the story. Your side characters can do that, too!

Activity: Create a side character who changes everything (50 words).

Example: A goofy friend reveals they're a secret agent, saving the hero from a trap. Describe their role and the surprising twist.

Villains with Depth

A lame villain kills a twist—like an evil overlord with no personality. Deep villains have motives readers can almost get behind, making twists more shocking. A villain's secret reason for being bad can turn your story into a legend!

Crafting Villains That Pop

- **Why One-Note Villains Fail:** Flat villains (e.g., "I'm evil for no reason") feel fake and ruin twists.
- **Motives Readers Get:** Give villains reasons, like revenge or saving someone, that make twists hit hard.
- **Twist-Friendly Villains:** A villain's secret motive (e.g., they're the hero's sibling) can be a game-changer.

Table: Flat Villain vs. Deep Villain

Type	Traits	Twist Potential
Flat Villain	No real motive, just "evil for evil's sake"	Weak twist (e.g., they're bad, obvious from the start)
Deep Villain	Has a relatable motive (revenge, justice, love, survival)	Strong twist (e.g., the villain turns out to be the hero's parent or mentor)

Example: In The Maze Runner, Ava Paige's motive (saving humanity) makes her villainy complex. A twist where she's tied to Thomas's past would've been wild! Your villains need that depth.

Prompt: Write a 100-word villain monologue revealing a twist motive. Example: A villain explains they stole a relic to save their family, not for power. Make their motive surprising but understandable.

✨ **Bonus:** Use the Free Character Profile Template (highlighted in the book description) to design multi-dimensional characters. It helps you map flaws, goals, and secrets for heroes, sidekicks, and villains to power your twists!

Favorite Characters for American Teens

Below is a table of characters from books, movies, and shows American teens love, showing their type (hero, sidekick, villain) and how they feel real, with twist potential to inspire your writing.

Table: Favorite Characters for American Teens

Character	Source	Type	How They Feel Real	Twist Potential
Katniss Everdeen	*The Hunger Games* (Book/Movie)	Hero	Stubborn, protective of family, struggles with trust	Peeta's fake betrayal shifts the story
Dustin Henderson	*Stranger Things* (Show)	Sidekick	Funny, loyal, nerdy, makes mistakes	His bond with Dart hides a dangerous twist
Draco Malfoy	*Harry Potter* (Book/Movie)	Villain	Arrogant but pressured by family expectations	His secret doubts could have flipped him to the hero's side
Percy Jackson	*Percy Jackson* (Book)	Hero	Loyal, sarcastic, feels like an outsider	His trust in Luke sets up a betrayal twist
Inej Ghafa	*Six of Crows* (Book)	Sidekick	Quiet, skilled, wrestles with past trauma	Her hidden strength drives Kaz's secret plan twist

Chapter Wrap-Up

Characters are the soul of your adventure, making your plot twists pop. By crafting relatable heroes, surprising sidekicks, and deep villains, you'll create stories as epic as The Hunger Games or Stranger Things. Use the tables, flowchart, mind map, prompts, and the Free Character Profile Template to build characters readers love. Ready to test your skills? Hit the quiz below and show you're a character-crafting pro!

Check Your Understanding: Character Twist Quiz

Time to see if you're a character-crafting genius! This quiz has 25 questions—5 of each type—to test your skills at creating heroes, sidekicks, and villains that power epic twists. From MCQs to short answers, show you've got what it takes! Answers are below each section—no peeking!

ACTIVITY ZONE

ACTIVITY 1 – MULTIPLE CHOICE QUESTIONS

1) Why are flaws important for a hero?
a) They make the hero perfect
b) They make the hero relatable and set up twists
c) They make the hero boring
d) They stop the story's action

2) Which character's courage as a sidekick sparks a twist in Harry Potter and the Deathly Hallows?
a) Ron Weasley
b) Neville Longbottom
c) Hermione Granger
d) Luna Lovegood

3) What makes a villain's twist more powerful?
a) Having no motive at all
b) Having a relatable motive that readers understand
c) Being evil just because
d) Ignoring the hero's story

4) How can a side character spark a plot twist?
a) By staying quiet and doing nothing
b) By revealing a hidden skill or betrayal
c) By having no personality
d) By repeating the hero's actions

5) What's a key trait for a hero's inner conflict?
a) It should confuse readers
b) It should lead to external surprises or twists
c) It should stop the story
d) It should be perfect and flawless

ACTIVITY 2 – TRUE/FALSE QUESTIONS

1. A hero's flaws make them less relatable to readers.
2. A side character's betrayal can spark a major plot twist.
3. A villain with no motive makes a twist more exciting.
4. A hero's inner conflict, like self-doubt, can lead to a story twist.
5. The Free Character Profile Template helps design twist-ready characters.

🎯 ACTIVITY ZONE

ACTIVITY 3 – FILL-IN-THE-BLANK QUESTIONS

1. A hero's _____ make them human and set up plot twists.
2. In Stranger Things, _____'s loyalty to Dart sparks a twist.
3. A villain's _____ should be relatable to make twists powerful.
4. A side character's _____ skill can surprise readers with a twist.
5. Inner _____ in a hero can lead to external story surprises.

ACTIVITY 4 – MATCHING QUESTIONS

Character	Twist Option
A. Katniss Everdeen (*The Hunger Games*)	1. Sidekick's courage shifts the battle
B. Dustin Henderson (*Stranger Things*)	2. Villain's motive ties to hero's past
C. Draco Malfoy (*Harry Potter*)	3. Ally's bond with a creature causes trouble
D. Percy Jackson (*Percy Jackson*)	4. Hero trusts a friend who betrays them
E. Inej Ghafa (*Six of Crows*)	5. Ally's secret strength drives a plan

ACTIVITY 5 – SHORT-ANSWER QUESTIONS

1. In 50 words, create a hero whose flaw leads to a plot twist. Example: A stubborn hero ignores a warning, triggering a trap.
2. In 30 words, describe a side character's hidden skill that sparks a twist. Example: The quiet friend reveals they're a hacker, unlocking a secret vault.
3. In 30 words, explain why a one-note villain weakens a twist. Example: A villain with no motive feels fake, making their twist (like a secret identity) boring.
4. In 50 words, write a villain monologue revealing a twist motive. Example: The villain stole a gem to save their sick sibling, not for power.
5. In 30 words, describe a hero's inner conflict that sets up a twist. Example: The hero's guilt over a past mistake hides their secret role in starting the war.

ANSWERS
🎯 ACTIVITY ZONE

(Use these to spark ideas, but make your answers 100% you!)

ACTIVITY 1: MCQ ANSWERS

1. b) They make the hero relatable and set up twists
2. b) Neville Longbottom
3. b) Having a relatable motive readers understand
4. b) By revealing a hidden skill or betrayal
5. b) It should lead to external surprises or twists

ACTIVITY 2: TRUE/FALSE ANSWERS

1. False (Flaws make heroes relatable)
2. True
3. False (No motive weakens twists)
4. True
5. True

ACTIVITY 3: FILL-IN-THE-BLANK ANSWERS

1. Flaws
2. Dustin
3. Motive
4. Hidden
5. Conflict

ACTIVITY 4: MATCHING QUESTIONS

1. A-4 (Katniss trusts Peeta, who fakes betrayal)
2. B-3 (Dustin's bond with Dart causes trouble)
3. C-2 (Draco's motive ties to his family's past)
4. D-4 (Percy trusts Luke, who betrays him)
5. E-5 (Inej's strength drives Kaz's secret plan)

ACTIVITY 5 : SHORT-ANSWER ANSWERS

1. Sample Answer: Mia, a reckless hero, ignores her team's warning, believing she's unbeatable. Her flaw leads her into a cave where a villain's trap reveals she's the villain's lost sister. (50 words)
2. Sample Answer: Sam, the shy sidekick, reveals he's a skilled pilot, flying the hero out of a collapsing ruin, changing the quest's path. (30 words)
3. Sample Answer: A one-note villain with no motive feels flat, so their twist (like being the hero's parent) lacks impact and fails to surprise readers. (30 words)
4. Sample Answer: "I stole the artifact to save my dying son," the villain growls. "You'd do the same for family. Hate me, but I had no choice." (50 words)
5. Sample Answer: The hero's fear of betrayal hides their secret: they once helped the villain escape, setting up a twist where they face their past. (30 words)

Chapter 4. Mastering Adventure Plot Structure

CHAPTER 4 – Mastering Adventure Plot Structure

Hey, teen writer! Ever wonder how epic adventures like The Hunger Games or Stranger Things keep you glued to the story from start to finish? It's all about plot structure—the roadmap that makes your adventure flow and your twists pop. In this chapter, you'll learn how to build a story that hooks readers, ramps up tension, and delivers killer twists, just like your favorite books and shows. Ready to map out your epic tale? Let's hit the road!

We'll dive into why structure is your storytelling superpower, how to craft a compelling beginning, middle, and end, where to introduce those game-changing twists, and how to maintain high energy. With examples, tables, a flowchart, mind maps, and fun prompts, you'll create a story that rocks. We'll wrap with a table of favorite stories American teens love, plus a quiz to test your skills. Let's make your adventure unstoppable!

Why Structure Is Your Storytelling Superpower

Plot structure is like a treasure map for your story—it guides readers through your adventure, keeping them hooked with twists and turns. A solid structure makes sure your hero's quest feels exciting, not messy, and sets up your plot twists to hit hard. Here's why it's key:

- **Roadmap to Success**: Structure keeps your story on track, from the hero's first step to the showdown.
- **Hooks Readers**: A clear beginning, middle, and end builds suspense and makes twists unforgettable.
- **Twist Amplifier**: The right structure places twists where they shock the most.

Example: In Percy Jackson: The Lightning Thief, the structure—meeting Percy, facing monsters, then Luke's betrayal—makes the twist hit hard. Your story needs that roadmap to shine!

Activity: Outline a 3-sentence adventure plot. Example: A teen finds a magic compass. They battle pirates to find a lost island. The island's a trap set by their missing sibling. Keep it short and twisty!

Beginning, Middle, and End

Every adventure follows a three-act structure: beginning (Act 1), middle (Act 2), and end (Act 3). Each act sets up your world, hero, and twists, keeping readers hooked. Let's break it down.

The Three Acts
- Act 1: World, Hero, Quest – Introduce your hero, their world, and the quest that kicks off the adventure (e.g., a mission to save someone).
- Act 2: Rising Tension and Mid-Point Twist – Pile on challenges and drop a game-changing twist halfway through to flip the story.
- Act 3: Climax, Final Twist, Resolution – Build to the big showdown, reveal a final twist, and wrap up the story.

Table: Three-Act Structure Breakdown

Act	Purpose	Example (The Hunger Games)
Act 1	Set up world, hero, quest	Katniss volunteers for Prim, enters the Games
Act 2	Build tension, mid-point twist	Training escalates; Peeta's fake alliance shocks
Act 3	Climax, final twist, resolution	Katniss and Peeta's berry trick wins the Games

Flowchart: Three-Act Adventure Structure

[Act 1: Introduce Hero/World] → [Quest Begins] → [Act 2: Challenges + Mid-Point Twist] → [Act 3: Climax + Final Twist] → [Resolution]

Example: Percy meets camp → Seeks lightning bolt → Luke's betrayal → Fights Ares → Saves Olympus

Example: In Harry Potter and the Sorcerer's Stone, Act 1 introduces Harry and Hogwarts, Act 2 piles on mysteries with a mid-point twist (the mirror's secret), and Act 3 delivers the climax (Quirrell's reveal as the villain). Your story needs this flow to make twists pop!

Prompt: Write a 100-word opening scene for your story's Act 1. Example: Your hero stumbles on a glowing map in their attic, sparking a quest to find a lost city. Set up the world, hero, and quest!

Where to Place Twists

Twists are the spice of your adventure, but where you put them matters. Drop them too early, and you spoil the suspense; too late, and readers might get bored. Let's nail the timing!

Twist Timing Tricks
- Early Reveals: Small twists in Act 1 (e.g., a hero's secret skill) set up bigger surprises.
- Mid-Point Reversal: A twist halfway through Act 2 (e.g., an ally's betrayal) flips the story's direction.
- Final Shocking Twist: A big reveal in Act 3 (e.g., the villain's true motive) caps the climax.

Mind Map: Plot Twist Placement

[Plot Twists]
    ├── Early Reveal: (Act 1, sets up stakes, e.g., hero's hidden power)
    ├── Mid-Point Reversal: (Act 2, flips story, e.g., ally's betrayal)
    ├── Final Twist: (Act 3, shocks at climax, e.g., villain's identity)
    ├── Impact: (Changes hero's path or resolution)

Example: In Stranger Things Season 1, an early twist (Eleven's powers) sets up the adventure, the mid-point twist (Barb's fate) shifts the tone, and the final twist (Will's rescue with lingering danger) seals the deal. Your twists need that strategic timing!

Activity: Plan a mid-point twist in 50 words. Example: Your hero trusts a guide to find a treasure, but the guide reveals they're leading them to a villain's trap. Describe the twist and how it changes the story.

Keeping the Story Moving

A great adventure never drags—especially in the middle! The "saggy middle" can bore readers, so you need to balance action, dialogue, and quiet moments to keep the energy high. Chapter length helps, too!

Avoiding a Boring Story

- Avoiding "Saggy Middle" Syndrome: Keep Act 2 exciting with new challenges, twists, or character reveals.
- Balancing Action, Dialogue, Quiet Scenes: Mix fast-paced fights, snappy talks, and reflective moments to maintain flow.
- Using Chapter Length for Energy: Short chapters for action, longer ones for reflection, keep readers hooked.

Table: Balancing Story Elements

Element	Purpose	Example (Six of Crows)
Action	Builds excitement	Heist scenes with traps
Dialogue	Reveals character/twists	Kaz's cryptic plans hint at secrets
Quiet Scenes	Deepens emotion	Inej reflects on her past
Chapter Length	Controls pace	Short chapters for heist, longer for planning

Example: In Six of Crows, the middle stays thrilling with heist action, witty banter, and quiet moments where Inej reflects, setting up Kaz's secret twist. Your story needs that balance to avoid a snooze-fest!

Prompt: Write a 50-word scene that shifts from action to reflection. Example: Your hero escapes a monster, then pauses to regret ignoring a friend's warning. Show the switch from high energy to a quiet, emotional moment.

Favorite Stories for American Teens

Below is a table of stories from books, movies, and shows American teens love, showing their three-act structure and key twist moments to inspire your writing.

Table: Favorite Stories for American Teens

Story	Source	Act 1 (Setup)	Act 2 (Twist)	Act 3 (Climax/Twist)	Key Twist Moment
The Hunger Games	Book/Movie	Katniss volunteers for Prim	Peeta's fake alliance shocks	Berry trick wins Games	Peeta's alliance was a ruse
Stranger Things (S1)	Show	Kids meet Eleven, seek Will	Barb's fate shifts tone	Will's rescue, lingering danger	Eleven's powers revealed early
Percy Jackson: The Lightning Thief	Book	Percy discovers demigod world	Luke's betrayal flips quest	Percy fights Ares	Luke's traitor reveal
Spider-Man: Into the Spider-Verse	Movie	Miles gains powers	Other Spider-People appear	Miles saves multiverse	Prowler is Miles's uncle
Six of Crows	Book	Kaz plans heist	Inej's capture raises stakes	Heist succeeds with cost	Kaz's secret plan saves Inej

Chapter Wrap-Up

Plot structure is your roadmap to crafting adventures that teens can't put down. By nailing the three acts, placing twists strategically, and keeping the energy high, you'll create stories as epic as Percy Jackson or Stranger Things. Use the tables, flowchart, mind map, and prompts to build your plot. Ready to test your skills? Hit the quiz below and show you're a plot structure pro!

🎯 ACTIVITY ZONE

ACTIVITY 1: MULTIPLE CHOICE QUESTIONS (MCQS)

1) What does Act 1 of an adventure story introduce?
a) The climax and final twist
b) The world, hero, and quest
c) The mid-point reversal
d) The resolution only

2) Which story has a mid-point twist where an ally's fake alliance shocks the hero?
a) Percy Jackson: The Lightning Thief
b) The Hunger Games
c) Stranger Things (Season 1)
d) Six of Crows

3) How does a mid-point twist in Act 2 help the story?
a) It wraps up the adventure
b) It flips the story's direction
c) It introduces the hero
d) It slows down the pace

4) What helps avoid "saggy middle" syndrome in Act 2?
a) Repeating the same scene
b) Adding new challenges or twists
c) Skipping to the climax
d) Removing all dialogue

5) How can chapter length affect story energy?
a) Long chapters always speed up the pace
b) Short chapters for action, longer for reflection
c) All chapters should be the same length
d) Chapter length doesn't matter

🎯 ACTIVITY ZONE

ACTIVITY 2: TRUE/FALSE QUESTIONS

1. Act 3 is where the hero is introduced to the story.
2. A mid-point twist can change the story's direction.
3. Quiet scenes should be avoided to keep the story exciting.
4. In Six of Crows, Kaz's secret plan is a final twist.
5. Short chapters can boost action scenes' energy.

ACTIVITY 3 : FILL-IN-THE-BLANK QUESTIONS

1. Act 1 introduces the hero, world, and _____.
2. In Stranger Things, the mid-point twist involves _____'s fate.
3. A _____ twist in Act 3 shocks readers at the climax.
4. To avoid a saggy middle, add new _____ or twists.
5. _____ scenes deepen emotion but need balance with action.

ACTIVITY 4 : MATCHING QUESTIONS

1–5. Match the story to its plot structure twist:

Stories:
1. A. The Hunger Games
2. B. Percy Jackson: The Lightning Thief
3. C. Stranger Things (Season 1)
4. D. Six of Crows
5. E. Spider-Man: Into the Spider-Verse

Twists:
1. Hero discovers they're a demigod
2. Ally's fake alliance shocks hero
3. Ally's secret plan saves someone
4. Prowler is hero's uncle
5. Barb's fate shifts the story

🎯 ACTIVITY ZONE

ACTIVITY 5 : SHORT-ANSWER QUESTIONS

1. In 50 words, write an Act 1 opening for an adventure story. Example: A teen finds a glowing map, sparking a quest.
2. In 30 words, describe a mid-point twist for a treasure hunt story. Example: The hero's guide reveals the treasure is a trap set by their sibling.
3. In 30 words, explain why a saggy middle weakens a story. Example: A saggy middle bores readers with no tension or twists, making them lose interest.
4. In 50 words, write a final twist for an adventure story's climax. Example: The hero's victory reveals the villain was their parent, protecting a secret.
5. In 30 words, describe a scene shifting from action to reflection. Example: The hero escapes a trap, then reflects on trusting the wrong friend.

ANSWERS
🎯 ACTIVITY ZONE

(Use these to spark ideas, but make your answers 100% you!)

ACTIVITY 1 – MCQ ANSWERS

1. b) The world, hero, and quest
2. b) The Hunger Games
3. b) It flips the story's direction
4. b) Adding new challenges or twists
5. b) Short chapters for action, longer for reflection

ACTIVITY 2 – TRUE/FALSE ANSWERS

1. False (Act 1 introduces the hero)
2. True
3. False (Quiet scenes deepen emotion)
4. True
5. True

ACTIVITY 3 – FILL-IN-THE-BLANK ANSWERS

1. Quest
2. Barb
3. Final
4. Challenges
5. Quiet

ACTIVITY 4 – SOCIAL VIBE SHARE

1. A. The Hunger Games → 2. Ally's fake alliance shocks hero
2. B. Percy Jackson: The Lightning Thief → 1. Hero discovers they're a demigod
3. C. Stranger Things (Season 1) → 5. Barb's fate shifts the story
4. D. Six of Crows → 3. Ally's secret plan saves someone
5. E. Spider-Man: Into the Spider-Verse → 4. Prowler is hero's uncle

ACTIVITY 5 – SHORT-ANSWER QUESTIONS

1. Sample Answer: Zara finds a glowing compass in her attic, pointing to a lost jungle city. She grabs her backpack, ready to uncover its secrets, unaware it's a trap. (50 words)
2. Sample Answer: The hero's map leads to a cave, but their guide admits it's a trap set by their rival, flipping the quest's goal. (30 words)
3. Sample Answer: A saggy middle lacks tension or twists, boring readers and making them skip pages, weakening the story's excitement and stakes. (30 words)
4. Sample Answer: As Jaden defeats the warlord, he learns she's his mother, guarding a portal to save their world, forcing him to rethink his victory. (50 words)
5. Sample Answer: Kai dodges lasers to escape a vault, then pauses, regretting ignoring his sister's warning about the traitor guide. (30 words)

Chapter 5. From Spark to Adventure: Brainstorming Ideas

CHAPTER 5 – From Spark to Adventure: Brainstorming Ideas

Yo, teen writer! Ever had a random idea—like a mysterious text or a weird dream—that felt like the start of an epic adventure? That's a story spark, and this chapter's all about turning those tiny ideas into full-blown tales packed with twists, like in Stranger Things or The Hunger Games. Brainstorming is your superpower for creating stories that hook readers. Ready to ignite your creativity? Let's dive in!

We'll explore how to find inspiration everywhere, use prompts and games to spark ideas, and organize your thoughts like a pro. With examples, tables, a flowchart, mind maps, and fun activities, you'll build adventures that pop. We'll wrap with a table of favorite story ideas from stuff teens love, plus a quiz to test your brainstorming skills. Let's turn your sparks into fireworks!

Why Brainstorming Is a Writer's Superpower

Brainstorming is like a treasure hunt for ideas—it takes a small spark and builds it into a wild adventure. Whether it's a "what if" question or a weird conversation you overheard, brainstorming helps you create stories with killer twists. Here's why it's your secret weapon:

- **Turns Sparks to Stories**: A single idea (e.g., a lost phone) can become a full quest with twists.
- **Unleashes Creativity:** Brainstorming lets you explore endless possibilities without rules.
- **Sets Up Twists:** Wild ideas lead to surprising plot turns that keep readers hooked.

Example: In Spider-Man: Into the Spider-Verse, the spark of "what if Spider-Man was a teen from Brooklyn?" became a multiverse adventure with the twist of Miles's uncle as the Prowler. Your ideas can grow that big!
Activity: Ask "What if?" five times to build an idea. Example: What if a teen finds a glowing key? What if it opens a secret portal? What if the portal leads to a trap? Keep asking to create a twisty adventure!

Finding Inspiration Everywhere

Ideas are all around you—dreams, news headlines, even random chats at school. The trick is turning these everyday moments into story seeds that grow into epic adventures with twists. Let's hunt for inspiration!

Inspiration Sources
- **Dreams:** Crazy dreams (e.g., fighting a shadow monster) can spark wild quests.
- **News:** Headlines (e.g., "Mystery Object Found") can inspire sci-fi adventures.
- **Overheard Conversations:** A snippet like "I saw it move!" can lead to a creepy twist.

Table: Turning Life into Story Seeds

Source	Example Spark	Story Seed
Dream	Chased by a glowing figure	Hero flees a ghost with a secret
News	"Lost hiker found"	Hiker uncovers a hidden city
Conversation	"He was acting weird"	Friend's odd behavior hides a betrayal

Flowchart: Spark to Story

[Real-Life Spark] → [Ask "What If?"] → [Add a Twist] → [Adventure Plot]

Example: Hear "I lost my phone" → What if it's cursed? → It controls minds → Quest to destroy it

Example: In Percy Jackson, Rick Riordan turned myths into a modern adventure by asking, "What if gods still exist?" The twist (Luke's betrayal) came from imagining a demigod's loyalty issues. Your sparks can do that, too!

Prompt: Write a 100-word story seed inspired by something you saw today. Example: You saw a creepy old house—write about a teen finding a secret door inside that leads to a twisty adventure. Make it vivid!

Prompts and Games for Creativity

Stuck for ideas? Prompts and games are like rocket fuel for your brain. Whether you're writing solo or with friends, these tricks spark scenes and twists that make your story pop.

Creativity Boosters

- **Solo Prompts**: Quick ideas like "A teen finds a map in their locker" kickstart scenes.
- **Pass-the-Story Game:** With friends, each adds a sentence to build a twisty tale.
- **Dice Rolls**: Roll a die to pick a theme (e.g., 1 = storm, 2 = betrayal) for instant inspiration.

Mind Map: Creativity Games

[Creativity Boost]
├── Solo Prompts: (Quick ideas, e.g., "A cursed necklace")
├── Pass-the-Story: (Group adds to plot, builds twists)
├── Dice Rolls: (Random themes, e.g., 3 = treasure)
├── Twist Potential: (Ideas spark surprises)

Example: In Six of Crows, a prompt like "What if thieves plan a heist?" led to Kaz's secret plan twist. A dice roll for "betrayal" could've inspired Inej's capture. Try these games to spark your own twists!

Activity: Roll a die (or pick a number 1–6) and write a 50-word scene. Themes: 1 = storm, 2 = betrayal, 3 = treasure, 4 = secret door, 5 = chase, 6 = mystery object. Example: For "storm," a teen battles a hurricane to save a glowing relic.

Organizing Adventure Ideas

Got a ton of ideas? Awesome! Now you need to organize them so your adventure doesn't turn into a mess. Notebooks, index cards, or digital tools can help, and storyboarding makes your quest feel like a movie.

Organizing Tricks

- Notebooks: Jot ideas in a dedicated journal for quick reference.
- Index Cards: Write scenes on cards to shuffle and rearrange.
- Digital Tools: Apps like Notion or Trello track plots and twists.
- Storyboarding: Draw key moments like a movie to visualize the adventure.

Table: Organizing Tools

Tool	Why It's Cool	Example Use
Notebook	Portable, creative	Sketch a hero's quest with twist notes
Index Cards	Flexible, rearrangeable	Card for mid-point betrayal twist
Digital Tools	Searchable, shareable	Trello board for plot and twists
Storyboard	Visual, movie-like	Draw hero finding a cursed map

Example: The Hunger Games feels like a storyboard—Katniss volunteering (Act 1), facing Careers (Act 2), and the berry twist (Act 3). Storyboarding your quest helps twists shine!

Activity: Draw a 5-box storyboard of key moments in your adventure. Example: Box 1: Hero finds a map. Box 2: Faces a monster. Box 3: Ally betrays them. Box 4: Climax battle. Box 5: Twist resolution. Sketch or describe each box!

Favorite Story Ideas for Teens

Below is a table of story ideas from books, movies, and shows teens love, showing their inspirational spark and twist potential to inspire your brainstorming.

Table: Favorite Story Ideas for Teens

Story	Source	Inspirational Spark	Twist Potential
The Hunger Games	Book/Movie	What if teens fight in a deadly game?	Ally's fake betrayal flips trust
Stranger Things (S1)	Show	What if a kid vanishes in a creepy town?	Girl's powers hide a lab secret
Percy Jackson: The Lightning Thief	Book	What if Greek gods exist today?	Friend's betrayal shocks hero
Spider-Man: Into the Spider-Verse	Movie	What if a teen becomes Spider-Man?	Uncle's villain role stuns
Six of Crows	Book	What if thieves plan an impossible heist?	Leader's secret plan saves ally

Chapter Wrap-Up

Brainstorming is your ticket to turning tiny sparks into epic adventures with mind-blowing twists. By finding inspiration everywhere, using prompts and games, and organizing ideas like a pro, you'll create stories as awesome as Percy Jackson or Spider-Man. Use the tables, flowchart, mind map, and activities to fuel your creativity. Ready to test your brainstorming skills? Hit the quiz below and show you're an idea-generating rockstar!

Check Your Understanding: Brainstorming Quiz

Time to see if you're a brainstorming genius! This quiz has 25 questions—5 of each type—to test your skills at turning sparks into twisty adventures. From MCQs to short answers, show you've got what it takes! Answers are below each section—no peeking!

🎯 ACTIVITY ZONE

ACTIVITY 1 – MULTIPLE CHOICE QUESTIONS (MCQS)

1) What's a key benefit of brainstorming for writers?
a) It limits your ideas to one story
b) It turns small sparks into full adventures
c) It skips the need for twists
d) It makes stories predictable

2) Which story's spark was "What if teens fight in a deadly game?"
a) Percy Jackson: The Lightning Thief
b) The Hunger Games
c) Stranger Things (Season 1)
d) Six of Crows

3) What's a good source for story inspiration?
a) Only boring textbooks
b) Dreams, news, or conversations
c) Repeating old stories
d) Ignoring real life

4) How can a dice roll game spark creativity?
a) It picks a random theme for a scene
b) It writes the whole story for you
c) It limits your ideas
d) It skips the need for twists

5) What's a benefit of storyboarding your adventure?
a) It makes the story longer
b) It visualizes key moments like a movie
c) It removes all twists
d) It replaces writing entirely

ACTIVITY 2 – TRUE/FALSE QUESTIONS

1. Brainstorming limits your creativity to one idea.
2. Overheard conversations can inspire story seeds.
3. A pass-the-story game is only for solo writers.
4. Storyboarding helps visualize twists in your plot.
5. In Six of Crows, the spark was a heist with a secret twist.

ACTIVITY 3 – FILL-IN-THE-BLANK QUESTIONS

1. Asking "_____" helps turn a spark into a story.
2. In Stranger Things, the spark was a kid vanishing in a _____ town.
3. A _____ roll can pick a theme like "betrayal" for a scene.
4. _____ cards let you rearrange scenes for your plot.
5. A _____ visualizes your adventure like a movie.

ACTIVITY 4 – MATCHING QUESTIONS

Story	Spark
A. *The Hunger Games*	1. What if a teen becomes Spider-Man?
B. *Percy Jackson: The Lightning Thief*	2. What if teens fight in a deadly game?
C. *Stranger Things* (Season 1)	3. What if thieves plan a heist?
D. *Six of Crows*	4. What if gods exist today?
E. *Spider-Man: Into the Spider-Verse*	5. What if a kid vanishes in a creepy town?

ACTIVITY 5 – SHORT-ANSWER QUESTIONS

1. In 50 words, write a story seed inspired by a dream. Example: A teen dreams of a glowing forest leading to a quest.
2. In 30 words, describe a "What if?" question for a twisty adventure. Example: What if a teen's phone starts predicting disasters?
3. In 30 words, explain why storyboarding helps writers. Example: Storyboarding visualizes key moments, making it easier to plan twists and keep the plot exciting.
4. In 50 words, write a scene for a dice roll theme (betrayal). Example: A friend reveals they sold the hero's map.
5. In 30 words, describe an idea from an overheard conversation. Example: "I saw it move!" becomes a teen finding a moving statue with a secret.

ANSWERS
ACTIVITY ZONE

(Use these to spark ideas, but make your answers 100% you!)

ACTIVITY 1 – MULTIPLE CHOICE QUESTIONS (MCQS)

1. b) It turns small sparks into full adventures
2. b) The Hunger Games
3. b) Dreams, news, or conversations
4. a) It picks a random theme for a scene
5. b) It visualizes key moments like a movie

ACTIVITY 3 – FILL-IN-THE-BLANK

1. What if?
2. Creepy
3. Dice
4. Index
5. Storyboard

ACTIVITY 2 – TRUE/FALSE

1. False (Brainstorming unleashes creativity)
2. True
3. False (It's a group game)
4. True
5. True

ACTIVITY 4 MATCHING QUESTIONS

1. A-2 (The Hunger Games: Deadly game spark)
2. B-4 (Percy Jackson: Gods exist spark)
3. C-5 (Stranger Things: Kid vanishes spark)
4. D-3 (Six of Crows: Heist spark)
5. E-1 (Spider-Man: Teen Spider-Man spark)

ACTIVITY 5 : SHORT-ANSWER QUESTIONS

1. Sample Answer: In a dream, Zara runs through a glowing jungle, finding a portal. It sparks a quest to stop a shadow king, but the portal hides a trap. (50 words)
2. Sample Answer: What if a teen's backpack holds a secret map that leads to a cursed city with a traitor guide? (30 words)
3. Sample Answer: Storyboarding helps writers visualize plot points, organize twists, and ensure the adventure flows like a movie, keeping readers hooked. (30 words)
4. Sample Answer: Leo trusts Mia, but she admits she sold their treasure map to bandits, betraying him for gold, forcing Leo to chase her to save the quest. (50 words)
5. Sample Answer: "It was glowing!" sparks a story where a teen finds a glowing stone in a park, hiding a secret that triggers a city-wide adventure. (30 words)

Chapter 6 : Writing Tricks to Hook Readers

CHAPTER 6 –Writing Tricks to Hook Readers

Yo, teen writer! Want to write an adventure so gripping that readers can't stop flipping pages, like in The Hunger Games or Stranger Things? It's all about writing tricks—killer first lines, suspense, dialogue, and emotional punches that make your plot twists pop. In this chapter, you'll learn how to hook readers from the first word and keep them begging for more. Ready to make your story a total page-turner? Let's dive in!

We'll cover tools to grab readers, how to build suspense, drop hints through dialogue, and balance action with emotion. With examples, tables, a flowchart, mind maps, and fun prompts, you'll craft stories that rock. We'll wrap with a table of favorite stories teens love, plus a quiz to test your hooking skills. Let's make your adventure impossible to put down!

Why Writing Tricks Hook Readers

Writing tricks are like cheat codes for keeping readers glued to your story. A strong opening, sneaky suspense, clever dialogue, and emotional depth make your twists hit harder and keep the pages turning. Here's why these tricks are your superpower:

- Grab Attention: A killer first line or cliffhanger sucks readers in.
- Build Suspense: Secrets and mysteries keep readers guessing about twists.
- Deepen Connection: Mixing action with emotion makes readers care, amplifying the impact of your twists.

Example: In Percy Jackson: The Lightning Thief, the opening line ("I didn't want to be a half-blood") hooks you, and Luke's betrayal twist lands because suspense and emotion build it up. Your tricks can do that, too!

Activity: Write a 50-word opening that screams adventure. Example: A teen bolts through a collapsing temple, clutching a glowing amulet as lasers fire. Make it fast-paced and twisty to grab readers!

Building Suspense and Mystery

Suspense and mystery are the fuel for epic adventures. Cliffhangers and secrets keep readers on edge, dying to know what happens next. These tricks set up your plot twists perfectly.

Creating Suspense

- Irresistible Cliffhangers: End scenes or chapters with questions (e.g., "Will they escape?") to force page turns.
- Secrets Fuel Curiosity: Drop hints about a character's past or a hidden danger to spark guesses.
- Pacing for Tension: Short sentences and quick scenes ramp up urgency.

Technique	Purpose	Example (*Stranger Things*)
Cliffhanger	Forces page turns	Will trapped in Upside Down
Secrets	Sparks curiosity	Eleven's mysterious powers
Pacing	Builds urgency	Quick cuts in chase scenes

Flowchart: Building Suspense to Twist

[Introduce Mystery] → [Drop Hints/Secrets] → [Cliffhanger] → [Plot Twist]
Example: Strange noise → Hero finds weird symbol → Trapped in cave → Guide's betrayal

Example: In The Hunger Games, Katniss hearing a scream in the arena (cliffhanger) builds suspense, hinting at danger and setting up Peeta's fake alliance twist. Your suspense can do that, too!

Prompt: Write a 100-word cliffhanger chapter ending. Example: Your hero is cornered in a jungle, hearing footsteps, only to see their best friend holding a villain's weapon. End with a question or a shock to keep readers hooked!

Dialogue That Drops Hints

Dialogue isn't just characters chatting—it's a sneaky way to foreshadow twists and make your story feel real. Good dialogue sounds natural but packs a punch with hints about what's coming.

Crafting Hint-Filled Dialogue

- **Foreshadowing Naturally:** Slip clues into casual talks (e.g., a friend's cryptic comment).
- **Realistic Yet Purposeful**: Make characters sound like teens, but every line moves the plot or hints at twists.
- **Subtle Hints**: Avoid obvious spoilers—tease secrets to build suspense.

Mind Map: Dialogue for Twists

[Dialogue]
 ├── Foreshadowing: (Hints at secrets, e.g., "I've seen that symbol before")
  ├── Realistic Tone: (Sounds like teens, e.g., slang)
  ├── Purposeful: (Moves plot or sets up twist)
  ├── Twist Impact: (Reveals betrayal, secret, etc.)

Example: In Six of Crows, Kaz's line, "I always have a plan," hints at his secret twist to save Inej. It's snappy, teen-like, and sneaky. Your dialogue can set up twists like that!

Prompt: Write 50 words of dialogue hinting at a secret. Example: A friend says, "You don't know everything about me," while clutching a locket. Make it natural but tease a twist!

Balancing Action with Emotion

Nonstop action is cool, but it can burn out readers like an endless video game level. Mixing action with emotional beats—moments of fear, hope, or regret—gives your story depth and makes twists hit harder.

Action and Emotion Balance

- Why Nonstop Action Fails: Too much fighting or chasing feels flat without heart.

- **Emotional Beats for Depth:** Show characters' feelings (e.g., guilt after a fight) to engage readers.

- **Twist Setup:** Emotions like doubt or trust amplify the impact of surprises (e.g., a betrayal hurts more).

Table: Action vs. Emotion

Element	Purpose	Example (Harry Potter)
Action	Drives excitement	Harry fights Quirrell
Emotion	Adds depth, sets up twists	Harry's fear of losing friends
Balance	Keeps readers hooked	Action (battle) + emotion (loss)

Example: In Spider-Man: Into the Spider-Verse, Miles's action-packed fight with the Prowler shifts to emotional shock when he learns it's his uncle. That mix makes the twist unforgettable. Your story needs that balance!

Activity: Write a 100-word scene mixing action and inner thoughts. Example: Your hero fights off drones, then panics about trusting a shady ally. Blend fast-paced action with emotional depth!

Favorite Stories for Teens

Below is a table of stories from books, movies, and shows teens love, showing their hooking techniques and twist moments to inspire your writing.

Table: Favorite Stories for Teens

Story	Source	Hooking Technique	Twist Moment
The Hunger Games	Book/Movie	Opening: Katniss's desperate volunteer	Peeta's fake alliance shocks
Stranger Things (S1)	Show	Cliffhanger: Will's vanishing	Eleven's powers hide lab secret

Story	Source	Hooking Technique	Twist Moment
Percy Jackson: The Lightning Thief	Book	Dialogue: Percy's "half-blood" line	Luke's betrayal flips trust
Spider-Man: Into the Spider-Verse	Movie	Action: Miles's spider bite	Prowler is Miles's uncle

Chapter Wrap-Up

Writing tricks like killer openings, suspense, hint-filled dialogue, and balanced action-emotion moments are your tools to hook readers and make twists pop. By mastering these, you'll craft adventures as epic as Percy Jackson or Stranger Things.

Use the tables, flowchart, mind map, and prompts to level up your writing. Ready to test your skills? Hit the quiz below and show you're a reader-hooking pro!

Check Your Understanding: Writing Tricks Quiz

Time to see if you're a hooking genius! This quiz has 25 questions—5 of each type—to test your skills at crafting page-turners with killer twists. From MCQs to short answers, show you've got what it takes! Answers are below each section—no peeking!

ACTIVITY ZONE
ACTIVITY 1 – MULTIPLE CHOICE QUESTIONS (MCQS)

1) What's the purpose of a strong opening line?

a) To summarize the whole story
b) To grab readers' attention instantly
c) To reveal the final twist
d) To slow down the pace

2) Which story uses a cliffhanger about a character vanishing?
a) The Hunger Games
b) Stranger Things (Season 1)
c) Six of Crows
d) Percy Jackson: The Lightning Thief

3) How does dialogue help with plot twists?
a) It slows down the story
b) It foreshadows secrets naturally
c) It avoids any hints
d) It replaces action scenes

4) Why does nonstop action burn out readers?
a) It lacks emotional depth
b) It's always exciting
c) It makes twists stronger
d) It replaces dialogue

5) What's a benefit of emotional beats in a story?
a) They remove all action
b) They make twists hit harder
c) They confuse readers
d) They skip the climax

ACTIVITY 2 – TRUE/FALSE QUESTIONS

1. A cliffhanger should always reveal the twist immediately.
2. Dialogue can hint at secrets to set up twists.
3. Nonstop action keeps readers hooked without emotion.
4. In Six of Crows, Kaz's dialogue foreshadows his secret plan.
5. Short sentences in action scenes build suspense.

ACTIVITY 3 – FILL-IN-THE-BLANK QUESTIONS

1. A _____ line grabs readers from the first word.
2. In Percy Jackson, Luke's _____ hints at his betrayal twist.
3. _____ scenes balance action to add depth.
4. A _____ ending keeps readers turning pages.
5. Dialogue should be _____ yet hint at twists.

ACTIVITY 4 – MATCHING QUESTIONS

Story	Technique
A. The Hunger Games	1. Dialogue hints at betrayal
B. Stranger Things (S1)	2. Action-packed spider bite
C. Percy Jackson: The Lightning Thief	3. Opening with desperate choice
D. Spider-Man: Into the Spider-Verse	4. Cliffhanger with vanishing
E. Six of Crows	5. Mystery with cryptic plans

ACTIVITY 5 –SHORT-ANSWER QUESTIONS

1. In 50 words, write an opening line and scene that screams adventure. Example: A teen grabs a glowing sword as alarms blare.
2. In 30 words, describe a cliffhanger ending for a chapter. Example: The hero's trapped as their ally holds a knife, smirking.
3. In 30 words, explain why emotional beats strengthen twists. Example: Emotional beats make readers care, so twists like betrayals hurt more and feel shocking.
4. In 50 words, write dialogue hinting at a secret twist. Example: "You don't know what I've done," she whispers, hiding a locket.
5. In 30 words, describe a scene mixing action and emotion. Example: The hero fights bandits, then regrets trusting a traitor friend.

ANSWERS
🎯 ACTIVITY ZONE

(Use these to spark ideas, but make your answers 100% you!)

ACTIVITY 1 - MCQ ANSWERS

1. b) To grab readers' attention instantly
2. b) Stranger Things (Season 1)
3. b) It foreshadows secrets naturally
4. a) It lacks emotional depth
5. b) They make twists hit harder

ACTIVITY 2 - TRUE/FALSE ANSWERS

1. False (Cliffhangers raise questions, not reveal twists)
2. True
3. False (Action needs emotion for depth)
4. True
5. True

ACTIVITY 3 –FILL-IN-THE-BLANK ANSWERS

1. Opening
2. Dialogue
3. Emotional
4. Cliffhanger
5. Realistic

ACTIVITY 4 – MATCHING QUESTIONS

1. A-3 (The Hunger Games: Katniss's volunteer opening)
2. B-4 (Stranger Things: Will's vanishing cliffhanger)
3. C-1 (Percy Jackson: Luke's dialogue hints)
4. D-2 (Spider-Man: Spider bite action)
5. E-5 (Six of Crows: Kaz's cryptic plans)

ACTIVITY 5 –SHORT-ANSWER ANSWERS

1. Sample Answer: "The cave's collapsing!" Zara snatches a glowing gem as rocks fall. She sprints through tunnels, heart racing, unaware the gem's curse will unleash a monster. (50 words)
2. Sample Answer: Kai hangs off a cliff, rope fraying. His best friend smirks above, holding a knife. "You trusted me?" he laughs, as the rope snaps. (30 words)
3. Sample Answer: Emotional beats build reader connection, making twists like betrayals or secrets hit harder by tying them to feelings like trust or fear. (30 words)
4. Sample Answer: "You think you know me?" Jake mutters, gripping a scarred key. "This stays buried." His eyes dart away, hiding his role in the city's destruction. (50 words)
5. Sample Answer: Mia dodges laser traps, heart pounding, then pauses, guilt hitting as she recalls ignoring her brother's warning about the traitor guide. (30 words)

Chapter 7. Beating Writer's Block and Staying Pumped

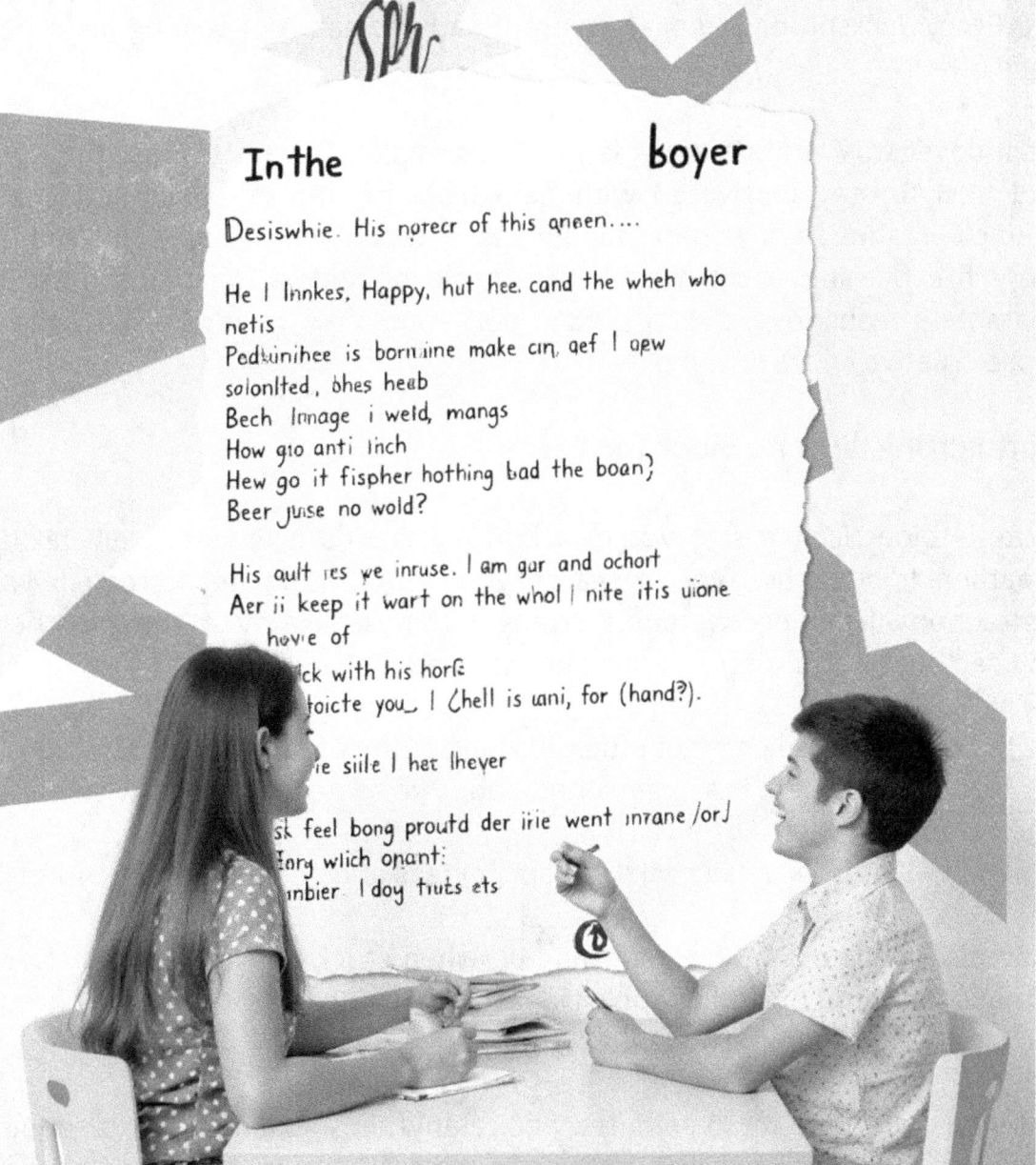

CHAPTER 7 – Beating Writer's Block and Staying Pumped

Yo, teen writer! Ever stare at a blank page, feeling stuck, like your epic adventure's gone poof? That's writer's block, and it happens to everyone—even pros who write stuff like The Hunger Games! This chapter's all about kicking writer's block to the curb and staying pumped to craft twisty stories like Percy Jackson or Stranger Things. Ready to get your writing mojo back? Let's dive in!

We'll cover why writer's block is totally normal, fun ways to bust through it, and how to stay motivated with help from friends or communities. With examples, tables, a flowchart, mind maps, and cool activities, you'll keep your story fire burning. We'll wrap with a table of motivational tips from fave characters teens love, plus a quiz to test your block-busting skills. Let's get those creative juices flowing!

Normalizing Writer's Block for Teens

Writer's block isn't a sign you're a bad writer—it's just your brain taking a breather. It hits when you're scared your story won't be perfect or when distractions (like binge-watching Stranger Things) take over. The good news? You can beat it and keep writing your twisty adventure!

- It's Normal: Even pros get stuck; it's part of the creative process.
- Motivation Is Key: Staying excited about your story (and its twists!) keeps you going.
- You've Got This: Small tricks can spark ideas and get you back to writing.

Example: Imagine J.K. Rowling giving up when stuck on Harry Potter. Nope—she pushed through, and Snape's twist became iconic! You can push through, too, and nail those plot twists.

Activity: Freewrite for 5 minutes about anything. Example: Write about a dragon, a random taco, or your hero's next twist. No rules—just let words flow to spark ideas!

Why Writer's Block Happens

Writer's block sneaks up for a few reasons, like fear, perfectionism, or distractions. Understanding why you're stuck is the first step to smashing through it and keeping your adventure on track.

Causes of Writer's Block

- Fear: Worrying your story won't be good enough (e.g., "What if my twist sucks?").
- Perfectionism: Trying to make every word perfect stalls your flow.
- Distractions: Social media, games, or stress can pull you away from writing.

Table: Why Writer's Block Hits

Cause	What It Looks Like	Example (Six of Crows)
Fear	Scared story isn't good	Kaz's heist plan feels "too simple"
Perfectionism	Rewriting same line	Obsessing over Inej's dialogue
Distractions	Phone, stress, games	Netflix binges stop heist writing

Flowchart: Why You're Stuck

[Writer's Block] → [Cause: Fear/Perfectionism/Distractions] → [Fix: Write Freely/Change Format/Find Support] → [Back to Twisty Story]

Example: Fear of bad twist → Try a 10-minute sprint → Write betrayal scene

Example: In Six of Crows, Leigh Bardugo might've feared Kaz's secret plan twist wouldn't land. But she kept writing, making it epic. You can beat fear, too!

Prompt: Write a 50-word pep talk from your hero to you. Example: Your hero says, "Hey, your story's gonna rock! Don't stress—just write that twist where I find the traitor." Make it encouraging!

Fun Fixes for Stuck Moments

Stuck on your story? No problem! Fun tricks like timed sprints or writing from your character's POV can blast through writer's block and spark new twists for your adventure.

Block-Busting Fixes

Timed Sprints: Write as fast as you can for 10 minutes—no editing!
Change Formats: Try a poem, script, or letter to shake things up.
Character POV Letters: Write as your hero or villain to explore their voice and spark twists.

Mind Map: Fixes for Writer's Block

[Writer's Block Fixes]
    ├──── Timed Sprints: (Write fast, no edits, e.g., 10 minutes)
    ├──── Change Formats: (Poem, script, list)
    ├──── Character Letters: (Write as hero/villain, e.g., reveal secret)
    ├──── Twist Spark: (New ideas for betrayals, secrets)

Example: In Stranger Things, a writer stuck on Eleven's arc might've tried a sprint, writing her escaping the lab, sparking the twist about her powers. Try these to unstick your story!

Activity: Do a 10-minute sprint writing a random scene. Example: A hero fights a robot in a junkyard, revealing a hidden chip. Just write—don't stop!

Finding Motivation Through Community

Writing's more fun with others cheering you on! Clubs, online groups, or events like NaNoWriMo (National Novel Writing Month) can keep you pumped. Sharing small wins—like a cool twist—boosts your vibe.

Community Motivation

- Clubs: Join a school writing club to swap ideas and twists.
- Online Groups: Find teen writer forums on sites like Reddit or Wattpad.
- NaNoWriMo: Write a novel in November with thousands of others.
- Share Wins: Tell a friend about your hero's betrayal twist for feedback.

Table: Community Motivation

Source	Why It Helps	Example (Percy Jackson)
Clubs	Swap ideas, get feedback	Share Percy's loyalty twist
Online Groups	Connect with writers	Post about Annabeth's role
NaNoWriMo	Write with a goal	Draft quest in 30 days
Sharing Wins	Boosts confidence	Friend loves Luke's betrayal

Example: Rick Riordan might've shared Percy Jackson drafts with a writing group, getting hyped for Luke's twist. You can find your crew to stay motivated!

Activity: Share a 50-word snippet with a friend for feedback. Example: Share your hero finding a cursed map, hinting at a twist. Ask what they think!

Motivational Tips from Favorite Characters

Below is a table of characters from books, movies, and shows teens love, showing their struggles and motivational strategies to inspire you to beat writer's block.

Table: Motivational Tips from Favorite Characters

Character	Source	Struggle	Motivational Strategy	Twist Inspiration
Katniss Everdeen	*The Hunger Games* (Book/Movie)	Fear of failure	Pushes through for Prim	Ally's fake betrayal twist
Eleven	*Stranger Things* (Show)	Feeling powerless	Trusts friends, keeps fighting	Powers hide lab secret
Percy Jackson	*Percy Jackson* (Book)	Self-doubt	Writes through loyalty issues	Friend's betrayal shocks
Miles Morales	*Spider-Man: Into the Spider-Verse* (Movie)	Inexperience	Tries new moves, persists	Uncle's villain role stuns
Kaz Brekker	*Six of Crows* (Book)	Perfectionism	Plans despite setbacks	Secret plan saves ally

Chapter Wrap-Up

Writer's block is no match for you! By normalizing it, using fun fixes like sprints and character letters, and finding motivation through community, you'll keep writing twisty adventures like The Hunger Games or Stranger Things. Use the tables, flowchart, mind map, and activities to stay pumped. Ready to test your block-busting skills? Hit the quiz below and show you're a writing rockstar!

Check Your Understanding: Writer's Block Quiz

Time to see if you're a block-busting pro! This quiz has 25 questions—5 of each type—to test your skills at beating writer's block and staying motivated. From MCQs to short answers, show you've got what it takes! Answers are below each section—no peeking!

ACTIVITY ZONE

ACTIVITY 1 – MULTIPLE CHOICE QUESTIONS (MCQS)

1) What's a common cause of writer's block?
a) Writing too fast
b) Fear of a bad story
c) Having too many ideas
d) Finishing a story early

2) Which character's struggle with self-doubt could inspire beating writer's block?
a) Katniss Everdeen (The Hunger Games)
b) Percy Jackson (Percy Jackson)
c) Eleven (Stranger Things)
d) Kaz Brekker (Six of Crows)

3) How can a timed sprint help with writer's block?
a) It slows down your writing
b) It forces you to write without editing
c) It skips the need for ideas
d) It makes you rewrite everything

4) What's a benefit of joining a writing community like NaNoWriMo?
a) It limits your writing time
b) It provides goals and support
c) It stops you from writing
d) It removes all twists

5) How does sharing a snippet help motivation?
a) It delays your writing
b) It boosts confidence with feedback
c) It makes you stop writing
d) It replaces your story

🎯 ACTIVITY ZONE

ACTIVITY 2 – TRUE/FALSE QUESTIONS

1. Writer's block means you're a bad writer.
2. A character POV letter can spark new ideas.
3. Perfectionism can cause writer's block.
4. In Stranger Things, Eleven's struggle inspires persistence.
5. Online writing groups can't help with motivation.

ACTIVITY 3 – FILL-IN-THE-BLANK QUESTIONS

1. _____ of failure can cause writer's block.
2. In Six of Crows, Kaz's _____ inspires pushing through setbacks.
3. A timed _____ helps you write without editing.
4. _____ groups like NaNoWriMo boost motivation.
5. Sharing a _____ with a friend builds confidence.

ACTIVITY 4 – FILL-IN-THE-BLANK QUESTIONS

Character	Source	Struggle	Motivational Strategy	Twist Inspiration
Katniss Everdeen	The Hunger Games (Book/Movie)	Fear of failure	Pushes through for Prim	Ally's fake betrayal twist
Eleven	Stranger Things (Show)	Feeling powerless	Trusts friends, keeps fighting	Powers hide lab secret
Percy Jackson	Percy Jackson (Book)	Self-doubt	Writes through loyalty issues	Friend's betrayal shocks
Miles Morales	Spider-Man: Into the Spider-Verse (Movie)	Inexperience	Tries new moves, persists	Uncle's villain role stuns
Kaz Brekker	Six of Crows (Book)	Perfectionism	Plans despite setbacks	Secret plan saves ally

🎯 ACTIVITY ZONE

ACTIVITY 5 – SHORT-ANSWER QUESTION

1. In 50 words, write a pep talk from your hero to beat writer's block. Example: "Don't quit—your twist is awesome!"
2. In 30 words, describe a timed sprint scene idea. Example: A hero fights a drone in a collapsing tower.
3. In 30 words, explain why perfectionism causes writer's block. Example: Perfectionism stalls writing by making you obsess over every word, stopping your flow.
4. In 50 words, write a character POV letter sparking a twist. Example: A villain writes about hiding a secret map.
5. In 30 words, describe a community motivation strategy. Example: Join NaNoWriMo to write with others and share twist ideas.

ANSWERS
ACTIVITY ZONE

(Use these to spark ideas, but make your answers 100% you!)

ACTIVITY 1 – MCQ ANSWERS

1. b) Fear of a bad story
2. b) Percy Jackson
3. b) It forces you to write without editing
4. b) It provides goals and support
5. b) It boosts confidence with feedback

ACTIVITY 2 – TRUE/FALSE ANSWERS

1. False (Writer's block is normal)
2. True
3. True
4. True
5. False (Online groups help motivation)

ACTIVITY 3 – FILL-IN-THE-BLANK ANSWERS

1. Fear
2. Perfectionism
3. Sprint
4. Writing
5. Snippet

ACTIVITY 4 – MATCHING ANSWERS

1. A-2 (The Hunger Games: Pushes through for Prim)
2. B-4 (Stranger Things: Trusts friends)
3. C-5 (Percy Jackson: Writes through self-doubt)
4. D-1 (Spider-Man: Tries new moves)
5. E-3 (Six of Crows: Plans despite setbacks)

ACTIVITY 5 – SHORT-ANSWER ANSWERS

1. Sample Answer: "Yo, don't stress!" Zara says. "Your story's gonna slay. Write that twist where I find the traitor's map. Keep going—you've got this!" (50 words)
2. Sample Answer: Jaden dodges lasers in a ruined lab, finding a glowing chip that hints at a traitor's plan. (30 words)
3. Sample Answer: Perfectionism causes writer's block by making you rewrite every line, fearing it's not perfect, which stops your creative flow. (30 words)
4. Sample Answer: "Dear diary," the villain writes, "I hid the map in the hero's bag. They'll never suspect I'm their sister, leading them to my trap." (50 words)
5. Sample Answer: Join a school writing club to share your betrayal twist and get feedback, boosting your motivation to keep writing. (30 words)

Chapter 8. Putting It All Together: Writing Your Adventure Stories

66

CHAPTER 8–Putting It All Together: Writing Your Adventure Stories

Yo, teen writer! You've nailed brainstorming epic ideas, crafting twisty characters, building killer plots, hooking readers, and beating writer's block—now it's time to flex those skills and write 10 adventure stories! This chapter is your ultimate story-writing workout, providing you with frameworks, including mind maps, flowcharts, and tables, to craft tales as gripping as The Hunger Games or Stranger Things. We'll guide you step by step through each story, then you'll write it yourself with an assignment prompt. Plus, you'll get a shadow prompt to remix the story with a new twist, character, or setting for extra practice. Ready to become a storytelling rockstar? Let's dive in!

We'll recap the skills from Chapters 1–7, then provide frameworks for 10 unique adventure stories. Each framework includes brainstorming, characters, plot structure, and twists/hooks, using tools to make writing fun and structured. You'll write the stories, and at the end, we'll share 10 sample stories to inspire you. We'll wrap with a table of favorite teen stories. Let's create some epic adventures!

Why This Chapter Is Your Story-Writing Workout

This chapter is where you put all your writing skills to work! You'll use brainstorming (Chapter 5), characters (Chapter 3), plot structure (Chapter 4), hooking tricks (Chapter 6), and block-busting tips (Chapter 7) to craft 10 stories with mind-blowing twists. Frameworks like mind maps and tables keep you on track, building confidence to write independently. Think of it like training for a quest—each story makes you a stronger writer!

- Recap Skills: Combine brainstorming, character depth, plot structure, and hooks for epic stories.
- Frameworks Rule: Tools like flowcharts guide you step by step.
- Practice Makes Perfect: Assignment and shadow prompts let you write and remix stories.

Example: Percy Jackson uses a clear structure (quest, betrayal twist) and hooks (Luke's cryptic dialogue). You'll use similar frameworks to make your stories pop!

Activity: Choose one skill from each chapter (1–7) and list how you'll use it in your stories. Example: Brainstorm with "What if?" (Ch. 5), craft a flawed hero (Ch. 3), use a cliffhanger (Ch. 6).

Story 1: The Cursed Compass Quest

Framework:
- Brainstorming Idea (Mind Map): Ask "What if a teen finds a cursed compass leading to a lost city?" Branch out: What if it's a trap? What if the villain's a relative?

```
[Cursed Compass]
    ├── What if it leads to danger?
    ├── What if it's cursed by a villain?
    ├── What if the hero's friend betrays them?
    ├── Twist: Compass hides a family secret
```

Character	Type	Flaw/Motive	Twist Potential
Hero (Ava)	Hero	Impulsive	Trusts compass, misses trap
Sidekick (Eli)	Sidekick	Overly loyal	Hides compass's curse
Villain (Mara)	Villain	Seeks power	Is Ava's lost aunt

Plot Structure (Flowchart):

[Act 1: Ava finds compass] → [Quest to lost city] → [Act 2: Faces traps, Eli acts weird] → [Mid-point twist: Eli knows curse] → [Act 3: Mara's trap] → [Final twist: Mara's her aunt] → [Resolution: Ava breaks curse]

Twists and Hooks (Mind Map):

```
[Twists/Hooks]
    ├── Cliffhanger: Ava trapped in city
    ├── Dialogue Hint: Eli says, "This compass feels wrong."
    ├── Emotion: Ava's fear of losing Eli
    ├── Twist: Mara's family tie
```

Assignment Prompt: Write a 500–800-word story about a teen finding a cursed compass leading to a lost city, with a betrayal twist. Use the mind map, table, and flowchart to guide you.

Shadow Practice Prompt: Rewrite a 300-word variation, changing the final twist (e.g., the compass is a test by Ava's parents).

Story 2: The Hidden Portal Betrayal

Framework:

- **Brainstorming Idea (Table):**

Source	Spark	Story Seed
Dream	Glowing portal in woods	Hero finds portal, ally betrays
News	"Mystery light in forest"	Portal hides villain's trap

Characters (Flowchart):

[Hero's Conflict: Feels alone] → [Meets sidekick] → [Sidekick's secret skill] → [Betrayal twist]

Plot Structure (Mind Map):

[Plot]
    ├── Act 1: Portal discovery
    ├── Act 2: Exploration, Mia's odd comment
    ├── Act 3: Mia betrays Sam
    ├── Balance: Action (portal chase), Emotion (trust issues)

Twists and Hooks (Table):

Element	Example
Cliffhanger	Hero trapped in portal
Dialogue Hint	"I've seen this place before…"
Twist	Sidekick works for villain

Assignment Prompt: Write a 500–800-word story about a teen discovering a portal, betrayed by an ally. Use the table, flowchart, and mind map.

Shadow Practice Prompt: Rewrite a 300-word variation, changing the sidekick's secret skill (e.g., time travel instead of hacking).

Story 3: The Shadow Monster Chase

Framework:

- **Brainstorming Idea (Flowchart):**

[Spark: Overheard "It moved!"] → [What if it's a monster?] → [Hero hunts it] → [Twist: Monster's a guardian]

- **Characters (Mind Map):**

[Villain-Monster]
    ├── Motive: Protect relic
    ├── Flaw: Too secretive
    ├── Twist: Is a guardian

- **Plot Structure (Table)**

Act	Key Moment	Twist
Act 1	See monster	Suspense builds
Act 2	Monster saves hero	Shifts goal
Act 3	Guardian reveal	Resolution

- **Twists and Hooks (Flowchart):**

[Mystery: Monster's shadow] → [Cliffhanger: Hero cornered] → [Twist: Monster's a guardian] → [Climax]

Assignment Prompt: Write a 500–800-word story about a teen chasing a shadow monster, with a guardian twist. Use the flowchart, mind map, and table.

Shadow Practice Prompt: Rewrite a 300-word variation, changing the hero's flaw (e.g., fearfulness instead of recklessness).

Story 4: The Forgotten Kingdom Heist

Framework:
- **Brainstorming Idea (Mind Map):**

[Heist]
├── What if teens steal a crown?
├── What if the kingdom is hidden?
├── Twist: Ally sabotages the heist

- **Characters (Table):**

Character	Type	Flaw/Motive	Twist Potential
Hero (Lila)	Hero	Impulsive	Misses ally's sabotage
Sidekick (Finn)	Sidekick	Ambitious	Sabotages for reward
Villain (King)	Villain	Protective	Hides kingdom's curse

- **Plot Structure (Flowchart):**

[Act 1: Plan heist] → [Act 2: Enter kingdom, Finn acts odd] → [Mid-point twist: Finn's sabotage] → [Act 3: Face king] → [Final twist: Crown's curse] → [Resolution]

- **Twists and Hooks (Mind Map):**

[Twists/Hooks]
├── Cliffhanger: Trap springs
├── Dialogue Hint: Finn says, "We'll be legends."
├── Emotion: Lila's trust issues
├── Twist: Crown's curse

- **Assignment Prompt:** Write a 500–800-word story about a teen heist in a hidden kingdom, with a sabotage twist. Use the mind map, table, and flowchart.
- **Shadow Practice Prompt:** Rewrite a 300-word variation, changing the villain's motive (e.g., saving kingdom instead of greed).

Story 5: The Time Loop Trap

Framework:
- **Brainstorming Idea (table):**

Tool	Idea	Twist Seed
Notebook	Reliving same day	Loop hides villain's plan
App	Time loop trap	Hero's stuck by ally

- **Characters (Flowchart):**

[Sidekick: Seems loyal] → [Hides skill: Time control] → [Twist: Sets loop trap]

- **Plot Structure (Mind Map):**

```
[Plot]
    ├── Act 1: Loop starts
    ├── Act 2: Find clues, tension
    ├── Act 3: Escape loop, twist
    └── Balance: Action (escape), Emotion (fear)
```

- **Twists and Hooks (Table):**

Element	Example
Cliffhanger	Loop resets at danger
Dialogue Hint	"You're not seeing it…"
Twist	Sidekick controls loop

- **Assignment Prompt:** Write a 500–800-word story about a teen trapped in a time loop, with a sidekick's trap twist. Use the table, flowchart, and mind map.

- **Shadow Practice Prompt:** Rewrite a 300-word variation, changing the early reveal (e.g., loop is a test instead of a trap).

Story 6: The Rebel Alliance Secret

Framework:
- **Brainstorming Idea (Mind Map):**

```
[Rebel Secret]
    ├── What if teens join the rebels?
    ├── What if the leader hides the truth?
    └── Twist: Leader's a spy
```

- **Characters (Table):**

Character	Type	Flaw/Motive	Twist Potential
Hero (Tara)	Hero	Justice-driven	Trusts leader
Sidekick (Rex)	Sidekick	Curious	Finds spy clues
Villain (Leader)	Villain	Power-hungry	Is a spy

- **Plot Structure (Flowchart):**

[Act 1: Join rebels] → [Act 2: Missions, clues] → [Mid-point twist: Rex finds clue] → [Act 3: Face leader] → [Final twist: Leader's a spy] → [Resolution]

- **Twists and Hooks (Mind Map):**

[Twists/Hooks]
├── Cliffhanger: Rebels ambushed
├── Dialogue: "Trust me, Tara."
├── Emotion: Tara's doubt
├── Twist: Spy reveal

Assignment Prompt: Write a 500–800-word story about a teen in a rebel alliance, with a leader-spy twist. Use the mind map, table, and flowchart.

Shadow Practice Prompt: Rewrite a 300-word variation, changing the emotional stakes (e.g., Tara's fear of losing family).

Story 7: The Enchanted Forest Mystery

Framework:

- **Brainstorming Idea (Flowchart):**

[Spark: "I saw it glow!"] → [What if forest is magical?] → [Hero investigates] → [Twist: Forest hides ally]

- **Characters (Mind Map):**

[Hero]
├── Conflict: Feels lost
├── Flaw: Doubts self
├── Twist: Ally in forest

- **Plot Structure (Table):**

Act	Key Moment	Twist
Act 1	Enter forest	Mystery grows
Act 2	Find ally	Shifts quest
Act 3	Ally's secret	Resolution

- **Twists and Hooks (Flowchart):**

[Mystery: Glowing trees] → [Cliffhanger: Hero lost] → [Twist: Ally's magical] → [Climax]

Assignment Prompt: Write a 500–800-word story about a teen solving a forest mystery, with an ally twist. Use the flowchart, mind map, and table.

Shadow Practice Prompt: Rewrite a 300-word variation, changing the mid-point reversal (e.g., ally is a villain).

Story 8: The Underwater Treasure Betrayal

Framework:

- **Brainstorming Idea (Table):**

Dice Roll	Theme	Twist Seed
2	Betrayal	Ally steals treasure
4	Secret door	Treasure hides trap

75

- **Characters (Flowchart):**

[Sidekick: Loyal diver] → [Hides betrayal] → [Twist: Steals treasure]

- **Plot Structure (Mind Map):**

[Plot]
├── Act 1: Dive for treasure
├── Act 2: Tension, traps
├── Act 3: Betrayal, climax
├── Balance: Action (dive), Emotion (trust)

- **Twists and Hooks (Table):**

Element	Example
Cliffhanger	Ship sinks
Dialogue Hint	"I know this wreck…"
Twist	Sidekick betrays

Assignment Prompt: Write a 500–800-word story about a teen diving for underwater treasure, with a betrayal twist. Use the table, flowchart, and mind map.
Shadow Practice Prompt: Rewrite a 300-word variation, changing the final twist (e.g., treasure is cursed).

Story 9: The Space Station Sabotage

Framework:
- **Brainstorming Idea (Mind Map):**

[Sabotage]
├── What if station malfunctions?
├── What if hero's blamed?
├── Twist: Ally sabotages

- **Characters (Table):**

Character	Type	Flaw/Motive	Twist Potential
Hero (Kai)	Hero	Overtrusting	Blamed for sabotage
Sidekick (Zoe)	Sidekick	Ambitious	Sabotages station
Villain (AI)	Villain	Control	Uses Zoe

- **Plot Structure (Flowchart):**

[Act 1: Station fails] → [Act 2: Kai blamed, Zoe acts odd] → [Mid-point twist: Zoe's sabotage] → [Act 3: Face AI] → [Final twist: AI's plan] → [Resolution]

- **Twists and Hooks (Mind Map):**

[Twists/Hooks]
├── Cliffhanger: Station explodes
├── Dialogue: "It wasn't me!"
├── Emotion: Kai's guilt
├── Twist: AI's plan

Assignment Prompt: Write a 500–800-word story about a teen on a sabotaged space station, with an ally twist. Use the mind map, table, and flowchart.

Shadow Practice Prompt: Rewrite a 300-word variation, changing the hidden skill (e.g., coding instead of engineering).

Story 10: The Lost Artifact Revelation

Framework:
- **Brainstorming Idea (Table):**

Tool	Idea	Twist Seed
App	Lost artifact found	Artifact reveals truth
Notebook	Hero seeks relic	Villain's tied to hero

- **Characters (Flowchart):**

[Villain: Seems evil] → [Monologue reveals motive] → [Twist: Villain's family]

- **Plot Structure (Mind Map):**

[Plot]
    ├── Act 1: Seek artifact
    ├── Act 2: Clues, tension
    ├── Act 3: Revelation, climax
    ├── Twists: Early, mid, final

- **Twists and Hooks (Table):**

Element	Example
Opening Line	"The artifact glowed…"
Cliffhanger	Hero trapped
Twist	Villain's family tie

- **Assignment Prompt:** Write a 500–800-word story about a teen finding a lost artifact, with a villain-family twist. Use the table, flowchart, and mind map.

- **Shadow Practice Prompt:** Rewrite a 300-word variation, changing the betrayal element (e.g., sidekick instead of villain).

Wrapping Up Your Storytelling Adventure

You've got the tools to write epic adventures! By using frameworks to craft 10 stories (and 10 shadow variations), you're mastering brainstorming, characters, plots, and twists. Keep using mind maps, flowcharts, and tables for your own tales. Share one story online or with friends to celebrate!

Final Motivation: Pick your favorite story and polish it using Chapter 7's tips, then share it to see readers flip over your twists!

Favorite Story Inspirations for Teens

Below is a table of stories from books, movies, and shows teens love, showing their frameworks and twists to inspire your writing.

Table: Favorite Story Inspirations for Teens

Story	Source	Framework Used	Twist Moment
The Hunger Games	Book/Movie	3-act structure, character table	Peeta's fake alliance
Stranger Things (S1)	Show	Mind map for mystery, flowchart for plot	Eleven's lab secret
Percy Jackson: The Lightning Thief	Book	Flowchart for betrayal, table for characters	Luke's traitor reveal
Spider-Man: Into the Spider-Verse	Movie	Mind map for action-emotion, table for hooks	Prowler's uncle twist
Six of Crows	Book	Flowchart for heist, mind map for twists	Kaz's secret plan

ANSWERS
SAMPLE STORIES

Here are 10 sample stories (150–200 words each) based on the frameworks, to inspire your writing. Each follows its framework exactly, showing how to apply the tools. Use these as a guide after writing your versions!

SAMPLE STORY 1: THE CURSED COMPASS QUEST (180 WORDS)

Ava, 16, found a glowing compass in her grandma's attic, buzzing with a strange hum. Her impulsiveness took over—she grabbed her backpack and dragged her loyal friend Eli into the jungle, chasing the compass's path to a lost city. Eli muttered, "This compass feels wrong," but Ava ignored him, dodging vines and traps. Spikes shot from ruins, and Eli confessed mid-way: "I knew it was cursed—your aunt Mara told me." Ava's heart sank as Mara, a power-hungry sorceress, emerged. "Welcome, niece," she sneered, revealing she'd cursed the compass to trap Ava and claim the city's power. Ava's fear of losing Eli fueled her. In the climax, she smashed the compass, breaking the curse. Mara vanished, freed from her own spell, and Eli apologized, shaken. Ava learned to temper her impulsiveness, emerging wiser as the ruins crumbled behind her. The adventure taught her to listen, turning her reckless streak into cautious bravery, ready for the next quest.

SAMPLE STORY 2: THE HIDDEN PORTAL BETRAYAL (160 WORDS)

Sam, 15, felt alone after moving to a new town. A dream of a glowing portal in the woods, sparked by a news story about a "mystery light," led him to investigate. His hacker friend Mia joined, excited. They stepped through the portal into a neon-lit city, but Mia's cryptic, "I've seen this place before," raised Sam's suspicions. Aliens chased them, and Mia locked the portal, smirking, "I work for them—this is my home." Sam's trust shattered, his loneliness hitting hard. Using Mia's forgotten gadget, he hacked a ship to escape, dodging laser blasts. The betrayal twist—Mia was an alien spy—forced Sam to rely on himself. Back home, he vowed to find real friends, his confidence growing. The adventure turned his isolation into strength, ready to face any portal—or betrayal—head-on.

SAMPLE STORY 3: THE SHADOW MONSTER CHASE (170 WORDS)

Jaden, 17, overheard kids whisper, "It moved!" sparking his reckless hunt for a shadow monster in city alleys. What if it's a beast? He tracked it, heart pounding, through dark corners. The monster, secretive and looming, saved Jaden from thieves in Act 2, shifting his goal from hunter to ally. Its glowing eyes hinted at a deeper purpose. In the climax, Jaden learned the monster guarded an ancient relic, cursed to protect it forever. A cliffhanger had him cornered, but the twist—it was a guardian, not a villain—changed everything. Jaden helped lift the curse, freeing the guardian. His recklessness became calculated bravery, learning to look beyond appearances. The adventure ended with the relic safe, and Jaden walked away stronger, ready to tackle any mystery with a sharper eye.

ANSWERS
🎯 SAMPLE STORIES

SAMPLE STORY 4: THE FORGOTTEN KINGDOM HEIST (190 WORDS)

Lila, 16, brainstormed a heist to steal a crown from a hidden kingdom, her impulsiveness driving the plan. She recruited Finn, ambitious for fame, unaware of his secret deal with bandits. They sneaked into the misty kingdom (Act 1), Finn muttering, "We'll be legends." In Act 2, traps sprung—spikes, nets—and Finn's sabotage became clear when he triggered a cage, smirking. Lila's trust issues flared, her heart racing. Facing the protective king in Act 3, the crown's curse revealed itself, binding Lila to the kingdom. Using her quick thinking, she outwitted Finn, breaking the curse with a hidden key. The king, grateful, let her go. Lila's impulsiveness turned into strategic courage, learning to question allies. The heist failed, but she emerged a legend for her bravery, ready for bigger adventures with a sharper sense of trust.

SAMPLE STORY 5: THE TIME LOOP TRAP (175 WORDS)

Kai, 15, jotted in his notebook about reliving the same day, trapped in a time loop. His sidekick Zoe seemed loyal, but her hidden time-control skill set the trap. Act 1: Kai woke repeatedly to alarms. Act 2: Clues piled up—Zoe's smirk, her odd "You're not seeing it…" Act 3: Zoe admitted she trapped Kai to protect a villain's plan. Fear gripped Kai, but he spotted her dropped device. In a heart-pounding climax, he rewired it, breaking the loop. The twist—Zoe's betrayal—taught Kai not to overtrust. His fear turned into resolve, escaping to a new day. Kai's adventure reshaped his naive trust into cautious strength, ready to face any trap with a clear head.

SAMPLE STORY 6: THE REBEL ALLIANCE SECRET (185 WORDS)

Tara, 17, joined a rebel alliance, driven by justice. What if the leader was a spy? Her curious sidekick Rex found clues—a coded message. Act 1: Tara trained with rebels. Act 2: Missions grew risky, Rex whispering, "Trust me, Tara," but his findings pointed to betrayal. A mid-point twist revealed the leader's coded orders. In Act 3, rebels were ambushed, and the leader confessed to spying for the enemy, power-hungry. Tara's doubt fueled her, rallying the team to outsmart him in a fiery climax. The spy twist hit hard, but Tara's leadership saved the day. Her justice-driven heart grew stronger, learning to question authority. The adventure left her ready to lead future rebellions with sharper instincts.

SAMPLE STORY 7: THE ENCHANTED FOREST MYSTERY (165 WORDS)

Mia, 16, overheard, "I saw it glow!" sparking a magical forest mystery. Feeling lost, her self-doubt pushed her to investigate glowing trees (Act 1). In Act 2, she met a mysterious ally, shifting her quest. The forest's magic trapped her in a cliffhanger, lost among vines. Act 3 revealed the ally's secret—they were a magical guardian hiding from hunters. Mia's doubt turned to courage, helping the guardian save the forest in a dazzling climax. The twist reshaped her view, turning self-doubt into confidence. Mia left the forest stronger, ready to tackle any mystery with newfound belief in herself.

ANSWERS
SAMPLE STORIES

SAMPLE STORY 8: THE UNDERWATER TREASURE BETRAYAL (180 WORDS)

A dice roll sparked Leo's underwater treasure hunt, diving with loyal Mia. Act 1: They explored a sunken ship. Act 2: Traps—sharks, collapsing decks—built tension, Mia saying, "I know this wreck…" In Act 3, Mia stole the treasure, betraying Leo to bandits. The ship began sinking, a heart-stopping cliffhanger. Leo's trust broke, but he used a hidden air tank to escape, outwitting Mia. The betrayal twist taught him to guard his heart. Leo surfaced, stronger, turning trust issues into sharp instincts for future dives.

SAMPLE STORY 9: THE SPACE STATION SABOTAGE (190 WORDS)

Kai, 16, faced a malfunctioning space station, blamed for sabotage. What if his ally Zoe did it? Act 1: Alarms blared. Act 2: Zoe acted odd, saying, "It wasn't me!" but clues pointed to her sabotage. Mid-point twist: Zoe tampered with systems for ambition. Act 3: Kai faced the AI villain using Zoe, with an explosion as a cliffhanger. Kai's guilt fueled him to rewire the station, stopping the AI in a tense climax. The twist—Zoe's betrayal—taught Kai not to overtrust. He saved the station, turning his flaw into strength, ready for any mission.

SAMPLE STORY 10: THE LOST ARTIFACT REVELATION (175 WORDS)

Zara, 15, used an app to note a lost artifact's glow, seeking it with passion. Act 1: She hunted the relic. Act 2: Clues piled up, tension rising. The villain's monologue in Act 3 revealed they were family, a shocking twist. A cliffhanger trapped Zara in a cave, but her quick thinking freed her, using the artifact's power to stop the villain. The family tie hit hard, but Zara embraced her heritage, resolving the conflict. Her adventure turned passion into wisdom, ready to face any relic hunt with a sharper heart.

We'd Love Your Feedback!

★ ★ ★ ★ ★

Please let us know how we're doing by leaving us a review.

Conclusion – Your Adventure Awaits: Keep Writing, Keep Twisting

Hey, teen writer—you did it! From that first "What if?" spark in the introduction to crafting 10 full adventure stories in Chapter 8, you've journeyed through the wild world of fiction writing. Remember why we started? Adventure storytelling isn't just about epic quests or jaw-dropping plot twists—it's about exploring who you are, expressing your voice, and connecting with others through stories that matter. You've unlocked the power of creativity (Chapter 1), mastered unforgettable twists (Chapter 2), built characters that leap off the page (Chapter 3), nailed plot structures that hook readers (Chapter 4), brainstormed ideas from everyday sparks (Chapter 5), added writing tricks to keep the pages turning (Chapter 6), beaten writer's block like a boss (Chapter 7), and put it all together in your own twisty tales (Chapter 8). That's not just a book you read—it's a toolkit for life.

Recap Your Superpowers:

- Creativity & Confidence: You learned how adventure stories spark imagination and build courage, from journaling your dream quest (Ch. 1) to finishing stories that tackle fears.
- Twists & Characters: Your heroes with flaws, sneaky sidekicks, and deep villains (Ch. 3) now power plot twists that surprise and stick, like those in Percy Jackson or Six of Crows (Ch. 2).
- Structure & Hooks: Three-act roadmaps (Ch. 4), cliffhangers, and emotional beats (Ch. 6) make your stories unputdownable, balanced with brainstorming games and sprints (Ch. 5 & 7).
- Putting It All Together: Those 10 frameworks in Chapter 8? They're your blueprint—now go remix them, share your stories on Wattpad or with friends, and watch readers gasp at your twists!

The Free Character Profile Template: Your Secret Weapon:

- Don't forget this bonus (grab it from the description)! Use it to flesh out heroes, sidekicks, and villains with motives, flaws, and twist potential. It's like a magic map for your next adventure—fill it out for one character today and see your story come alive.

Your Call to the Next Adventure:

- You're the hero now. Writing isn't about perfection—it's about finishing, sharing, and growing. Tackle that writer's block with a 5-minute freewrite (Ch. 7), brainstorm a new "What if?" (Ch. 5), and outline your dream story (Ch. 4). The world needs your voice—your twists, your worlds, your adventures.
- Final Prompt: Write a 200-word epilogue to one of your Chapter 8 stories. What happens after the final twist? Does your hero face a new quest, or reflect on their growth? Share it online and tag it #TeenTwistTales—let's build a community of young storytellers!

You started this book as a dreamer; now you're a doer. Keep writing, keep twisting, keep adventuring. The blank page is your portal—what's next? Go make it epic!

The End… Or Is It? (Hint: Your story's just beginning!)

Appendix

APPENDIX -A : PLOT TWIST TYPES AND PLACEMENT GUIDE

A quick reference for crafting unforgettable twists, based on Chapters 2 and 4. Use this to decide where to drop your surprises in the three-act structure.

Twist Type	Description	Best Placement	Example from Book	Teen Tip
Betrayal Twist	An ally turns traitor, hitting emotional stakes.	Mid-Point (Act 2)	Luke in *Percy Jackson*	Make it hurt—readers love the shock!
Family Secret	Hero discovers a relative's hidden role.	Final (Act 3 Climax)	Mara as Ava's aunt (*Story 1*)	Tie it to the hero's flaw for depth.
Guardian Reveal	Enemy is actually a protector.	Mid-Point Reversal	Shadow monster in *Story 3*	Flip expectations—keep clues subtle.
Cursed Object	Item leads to trap or power.	Early (Act 1)	Cursed compass in *Story 1*	Build curiosity with hints in dialogue.
Time Loop Trap	Repeating events hide a bigger plot.	Act 2 Tension	Zoe's loop in *Story 5*	Use emotion to avoid repetition burnout.

APPENDIX -B : CHARACTER CREATION QUICK-REFERENCE TEMPLATE

Inspired by Chapter 3 and the Free Character Profile Template bonus. Fill this in for heroes, sidekicks, or villains to make them twist-ready.

Character Element	Hero Example (e.g., Ava)	Sidekick Example (e.g., Eli)	Villain Example (e.g., Mara)	Twist Tie-In
Name & Age	Ava, 16	Eli, 16	Mara, 40	N/A
Flaw / Struggle	Impulsive, trusts too easily	Overly loyal, hides secrets	Power-hungry, family guilt	Flaw leads to betrayal twist
Goal / Motive	Find lost city for adventure	Protect friend from danger	Claim compass power	Motive reveals family secret
Key Trait	Brave but reckless	Tech-savvy, secretive	Manipulative, magical	Trait hints at guardian role
Twist Potential	Discovers relative	Knows curse but stays silent	Is hero's aunt	Powers the mid-point reversal

APPENDIX -C : THREE-ACT STRUCTURE CHECKLIST

From Chapter 4—your roadmap to balanced plots. Check off as you outline to avoid saggy middles and amp up twists.

Act	Key Elements	Twist/Hook Opportunity	Example from Book	Quick Check
Act 1 (Beginning, 25% of story)	Introduce world, hero, quest; hook with opening line.	Early reveal (e.g., secret skill).	Ava finds compass (Story 1).	Does it grab attention? ☐
Act 2 (Middle, 50% of story)	Rising tension, challenges, mid-point reversal.	Mid-point twist (e.g., betrayal).	Eli confesses curse (Story 1).	Balance action/emotion? ☐
Act 3 (End, 25% of story)	Climax, final twist, resolution; emotional payoff.	Final shocking twist (e.g., family secret).	Mara's aunt reveal (Story 1).	Satisfying close? ☐

APPENDIX -D : BRAINSTORMING AND HOOKING TOOLS AT A GLANCE

Pull from Chapters 5 and 6 for sparking ideas and keeping readers hooked. Use this during freewrites or sprints to beat block (Ch. 7).

Tool	How to Use	Twist/Hook Focus	Example Prompt	Pro Tip
"What If?" Mind Map	Branch 5 ideas from a spark (e.g., cursed object).	Sparks betrayal or guardian twist.	What if the portal leads to a trap? (Story 2)	Add emotion for depth.
Dice Roll Game	Roll for theme (1 = storm, 2 = betrayal) and write 50 words.	Builds suspense for cliffhangers.	Roll 2: Betrayal in dive (Story 8).	Remix for shadow practice.
Cliffhanger Checklist	End scene with a question (e.g., "Who's the traitor?").	Fuels curiosity for mid-point reversal.	Hero trapped in city (Story 1).	Read aloud to test punch.
Dialogue Hint Table	List 3 lines foreshadowing a secret.	Natural setup for family reveal.	"This feels wrong…" (Eli in Story 1).	Keep it teen-realistic.
Freewrite Sprint	Write 5 mins on anything, no edits.	Overcomes perfectionism block.	Random scene: Hero vs. monster (Ch. 7).	Use for shadow variations.

APPENDIX -E : BEATING BLOCK & SHARING YOUR STORIES

From Chapters 7 and 8—motivation and publishing tips. Use this when stuck or ready to share your twisty tales.

Challenge	Quick Fix	Twist Tie-In	Example	Next Step
Writer's Block (Fear)	Pep talk from hero (50 words).	Hero encourages twist writing.	Ava: "Don't quit—your curse twist rocks!" (Ch. 7)	Freewrite 5 mins.
Perfectionism	Timed sprint (10 mins, no edits).	Practice mid-point betrayal.	Write Zoe's loop trap (Story 5).	Share snippet with friend.
Motivation Dip	Join NaNoWriMo or Wattpad group.	Get feedback on spy twist.	Post rebel alliance teaser (Story 6).	Track reactions online.
Sharing Anxiety	Write back cover blurb (50 words).	Tease family secret.	"Niece vs. aunt in cursed city" (Story 1).	Post 50-word teaser safely.
Feedback Overload	Ask specific questions (e.g., "Does twist surprise?").	Refine guardian reveal.	"Is monster twist too obvious?" (Story 3).	Edit and remix shadow version.

YOUNG WRITER SERIES - DR. FANATOMY

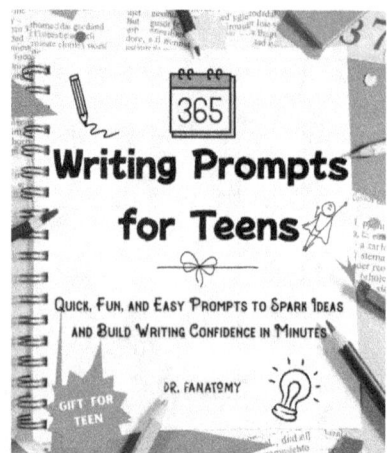

www.ingramcontent.com/pod-product-compliance
Lightning Source LLC
Chambersburg PA
CBHW081405070526
44583CB00020B/2683